It's hard to avoid the expec
'deliver' constant self-fulfi
appointment. Paul Mallai

fallen world, but then demonstrates from Scripture and from his own experience that disappointments are designed by our loving and all-Sovereign God to draw us into deeper intimacy with himself. There is much practical biblical counsel on how to respond to frustration and disappointment (whether in our work, our relationships, our church, with ourselves or with God himself). All the way through, we are pointed to the time when God will release creation from frustration and bondage, and restore all things to how they were meant to be.
Dr Sharon James, Policy Analyst, The Christian Institute, Newcastle upon Tyne

This is a book that was lived out before it was written. As a father and grandfather, along with his wife Edrie, Paul Mallard knows a loss that will never be made up in this world. As a pastor, he has counselled hundreds in the variety of their fears and disappointments. As a preacher, deeply engaged with Scripture and alight with the joy of knowing Christ, he knows the glorious future that is before us all.
Peter Lewis, author, conference speaker and former pastor of Cornerstone Church, Nottingham, UK

Disappointments at some point invade most areas of our lives. Paul Mallard writes honestly and realistically about these, and encourages us not to avoid them, remove them or escape from them but to embrace them, and to find that there is a place of refuge and meaning within them. Every disappointment becomes an opportunity to grow more deeply in God.
Charles Price, Senior Pastor, The People's Church, Toronto, Ontario, Canada

The best comfort in life comes from those who've needed the comfort they're sharing themselves. In this short but profound book, Paul Mallard wonderfully shares the stories, hymns, poems and books that have helped him to live with disappointment, and that – most of all – point us to the Sovereign God who will soon replace all the disappointments of this world with complete and eternal satisfaction in Him.

Ed Shaw, Pastor of Emmanuel City Centre, Bristol, and author of The Plausibility Problem

Invest Your Disappointments

Invest Your Disappointments

Going for Growth

PAUL MALLARD

INTER-VARSITY PRESS
36 Causton Street, London SW1P 4ST, England
Email: ivp@ivpbooks.com
Website: www.ivpbooks.com

First published 2018

British Library Cataloguing-in-Publication Data
A catalogue record for this book is available from the British Library.

ISBN: 978–1–78359–445–0
eBook ISBN: 978–1–78359–562–4

Set in Dante 11.5 pt/14 pt
Typeset in Great Britain by CRB Associates, Potterhanworth, Lincolnshire
Printed in Great Britain by Ashford Colour Press Ltd, Gosport, Hampshire

Inter-Varsity Press publishes Christian books that are true to the Bible and that communicate the gospel, develop discipleship and strengthen the church for its mission in the world.

IVP originated within the Inter-Varsity Fellowship, now the Universities and Colleges Christian Fellowship, a student movement connecting Christian Unions in universities and colleges throughout Great Britain, and a member movement of the International Fellowship of Evangelical Students. Website: www.uccf.org.uk. That historic association is maintained, and all senior IVP staff and committee members subscribe to the UCCF Basis of Faith.

Dedicated to Esme, Ivy, Avennah, Evangeline ('Genie'),
Moses, Opal and Abraham

'Grandchildren are the crown of the aged'
(Proverbs 17:6 ESV)

Contents

Home at last

Foreword

Like you, I'm no stranger to disappointment. It even features in my Facebook profile: 'Joyful Christian, lucky husband, proud dad/grandad, privileged pastor and permanently disappointed follower of Ipswich Town Football Club'. I imagine that our author, as a supporter of West Bromwich Albion, understands this feeling well!

But seriously, what is disappointment? Paul Mallard defines it as 'the sadness experienced when people or circumstances do not fulfil our expectations' (chapter 2). It's the difference between what is and what we had hoped would be. Which makes disappointment an essential element of the human condition; it touches every aspect of life.

Anyone who knows Paul and Edrie will realize that they are no strangers to disappointment. Drawing from the deep well of personal experience and skilfully mining rich seams of theological gold, Paul maps out the contours of the Land of Disappointment. With a warm heart and open Bible, he explores the bewildering array of disappointments we face in life – with ourselves, with our family, in marriage, in church and, ultimately, with God himself. With disarming honesty and not a little humour, Paul helps us to see that it's OK to feel disappointed. Life in the Garden was never meant to be this way. Above all, he reminds us that disappointment won't have the final word.

So, if disappointment is part of the warp and woof of life east of Eden, what is it for? This is an important question because disappointment not only robs us of our joy; at its worst, it can shipwreck our faith. So what are we supposed to do with it? Paul gives us the clue in the title of this book: the secret is to invest it wisely. To see God's hand at work and allow it to shape our attitudes and mould our desires. Far from being an enemy to be feared, disappointment invested well will drive us into the arms of God. At best, it will make us hungry for him and homesick for heaven.

Writing with warmth, insight and sensitivity, Paul doesn't lecture us. Rather, he sits down beside us and, like the true pastor he is, gives expression to our fears. It feels as if *Invest Your Disappointments* has been written by an understanding friend.

Paul reads widely and thinks deeply, but he always wears his learning lightly. He moves freely between Martin Luther, John Calvin and Tim Keller on the one hand and T. S. Eliot, William Shakespeare and Dag Hammarskjöld on the other. Above all, the author enjoys quoting from C. S. Lewis, so I'll finish with a C. S. Lewis quotation of my own, taken from *The Last Battle*:

> Now at last they were beginning Chapter One of the Great Story which no one on earth has read: which goes on for ever: in which every chapter is better than the one before.[1]

But, like Paul, let's leave the last word to God himself:

> For the Lamb at the centre of the throne will be their shepherd;
>   'he will lead them to springs of living water.'
>   'And [I] will wipe away every tear from their eyes.'
> (Revelation 7:17)

Richard Underwood
former Pastoral Director
Fellowship of Independent Evangelical Churches

Introduction

Carrying the tears inside . . .

He was going to be called Nathan.

After a five-year courtship and a six-month engagement, I married Edrie, my childhood sweetheart. I got a job as a religious education teacher, and we moved into our first home in Wiltshire. The first year was crowned with the exciting discovery that Edrie was pregnant.

We had already decided that we wanted a large family: I said five; Edrie preferred six. We couldn't wait to tell everyone – this would be the first grandchild. My dad cried and my mum made a cup of tea. Edrie's parents prayed, and her dad anticipated a new phase in his family history research.

We told a few friends. Others found out and sent us congratulations. We attended antenatal classes. The date for the birth was set: 23 April, St George's Day. We began to dream. We agreed on names.

He would be called Nathan.

And then, in the middle of a cold winter's night, Edrie began to experience severe pains. We saw the doctor the next day and he admitted her to hospital. She wept as the consultant told us that our baby was gone. He assured us that there were no long-term complications, and having children in the future would be a real possibility.

But his assurances seemed hollow.

Edrie was devastated. She had to have minor surgery, and they gave her strong painkillers – but nothing could touch the emotional pain she felt at the loss of our first child. Her body had prepared her for something that would never happen.

And that's what it felt like – the loss of a child. We never actually met Nathan, but he was already part of our lives. And, of course, with grief comes a whole series of irrational feelings and distressing questions. What had we done wrong? Were we being punished? Why had God allowed us to experience joy and sorrow in such intimate proximity? Would we really be able to have children? Would we ever be happy again? We were embarrassed about telling people and felt guilty about our fears.

Miscarriage is a particular kind of loss, and it is easy to minimize it. You are grieving for a person you never knew and for a relationship that ended before it really began. We had lost a baby – even the words sound strange, curiously like carelessness. It's a kind of hidden tragedy, like something to be ashamed of. You carry the tears inside.

Nathan left us thirty-five years ago, at the time of writing – that's half a lifetime. Edrie experienced two more miscarriages, but we now have four children and numerous grandchildren. However, Edrie still feels a kind of wistful sadness. April 23rd never comes around without her reminding me that it would have been Nathan's birthday.

I guess that it was our first real experience of how bitter disappointment could be.

Of course, we had both experienced it many times before. I remember the moment when it dawned on me that I would never be a centre forward for West Bromwich Albion – I was six at the time! Edrie regretted never getting to see a live perform-ance of Abba, her favourite pop group. But these are minor things – we look back and even laugh about them. This was real. This would affect our lives for ever.

Disappointment is part of the universal human condition.

It is the sadness we feel when our hopes are shattered and our expectations fail to be realized. It is a subjective response to painful circumstances. It can easily lead to disillusionment, disenchantment and discouragement. In extreme circumstances it may even result in a collapse of faith.

We cannot avoid disappointment, but how do we avoid being paralysed by it? And what can we learn from it?

Of course, disappointment can be extremely painful, paralysing even. Yet, at the same time, it can become a source of growth and a spur to maturity. It is unhealthy to brush painful feelings under the carpet – the Bible never does so. Instead, it meets them head-on, and so must we.

If God folds disappointment into the texture of our lives, then it is for a purpose. Understanding ourselves, and the causes of our disappointments, will give us perspective and courage. Grasping something of God's purpose will give us patience and hope.

The way in which our hearts react to disappointments will determine the direction of our lives. If we allow grumbling and criticism to grip our hearts, we will struggle with disappointment and allow it to shape our whole outlook. If, on the other hand, we cultivate a grateful, thankful heart, we will learn to deal with disappointments in a God-honouring way.

In this book we will take a journey through the Land of Disappointment. The landscape will be familiar to all of us, though we may come upon some yet-undiscovered vistas. On the way we will discover strength to continue the journey. The greatest comfort of all will be to look beyond our current pilgrimage to what hymn writer Isaac Watts called 'a land of pure delight'.[1] There our desires will be purified, our expectations realized and our hearts will be eternally satisfied. Disappointment will be gone for ever.

I hope that the help you will find here will be solidly biblical – in the end our greatest balm of all is the medicine found in Scripture. I also hope you benefit from the pastoral insights and practical applications that decades of people helping have afforded me.

Each chapter concludes with a series of questions, for personal reflection or to aid group discussion. When we talk about our disappointments with others, we very quickly discover that we are not alone.

May the God of all comfort, comfort us in all our troubles, 'so that we can comfort those in any trouble with the comfort we ourselves receive from God. For just as we share abundantly in the sufferings of Christ, so also our comfort abounds through Christ' (2 Corinthians 1:4–5).

Interwoven with the journey or travelling metaphor is that of banking and wise investment. How can we invest our experience of travelling through the Land of Disappointment in a healthy way so that it will pay rich dividends?

Let's prepare for the journey ahead. Let's be courageous and intentional about our investment of disappointment as we aim for healthy, lasting growth.

Preparing
for the journey

1. Living outside the Garden

Last Christmas was the first one that my mum spent in a care home.

My earliest memories of Christmas focus on my parents. My dad worked in an old-fashioned grocer's shop and so Christmas Eve was incredibly busy for him. He would shut up shop late in the afternoon and then cycle home. My sister and I watched eagerly for his return. He would park his bike and come in with frost in his hair and a twinkle in his eyes.

'Do you want to see what I've got in my pocket?' he'd ask.

And of course we always did! There we would find once-a-year Christmas delights – cashew nuts and satsumas and chocolate coins.

That was when Christmas truly began.

But Christmas was really about my mum. She was the general commanding the whole campaign. She was the one who was always unflustered and unperturbed. Amidst excited kids and exasperated dads and excruciating relatives, she was the calm at the heart of the maelstrom.

I guess she was always like that. Mum was the typical working-class matriarch – able to cope with most things that life threw at her. She grew up in the grim days of the Second World War. My dad returned from North Africa in 1945, and they married a few months later. An old black-and-white photograph of their wedding day still captures a long-ago bubble of happiness and hope.

Mum brought up the family on meagre means, doing menial jobs to give us a few luxuries. She nursed both her parents in their final illnesses. I grew up with the security of her competence, capability and kindness. She was all about sacrifice and love. I can never remember her actually telling me that she loved me, but I never doubted it for a moment. The only time I saw her cry was when we stood at Dad's bedside after the one love of her life had departed this world at the ridiculously young age of sixty.

Mum could cope with anything.

But not any more. Dementia took up unwelcome residency a couple of years ago.

Mixed emotions

Sometimes it's hilarious.

My sister recently arrived at the home to be told that yesterday had been a really exciting day.

'Why was it exciting, Mum?'

'Because we had a really important visitor.'

'Who was that, Mum?'

'It was Mr Churchill.'

'What! Do you mean Winston Churchill . . . from the war?'

'Yes, Mr Churchill.'

'Wow! That *was* exciting, Mum. Did he smoke one of his big cigars?'

(Accompanied by a look of profound consternation) 'Don't be so silly. He couldn't smoke in here. It's a care home!'

Sometimes it's hilarious – but most of the time it is just profoundly distressing.

Mum now lives in that twilight world between memory and reality. Every day she fights a battle with confusion and bewilderment. Our memories make us the people we are, and Alzheimer's cruelly steals those memories away. If God gave us memory so 'that we might have roses in December',[1] then a loss of memory means that those roses never bloom.

I miss my mum so much. Bits of her are still there: that knowing look or the raised eyebrow. But much of her is gone. I sometimes look into uncomprehending eyes and think, 'Somewhere in there is my mum.'

My mum has gone, and the disappointment caused by her loss will accompany me for the rest of my life.

Why?

Why is the world like this? Why does disappointment dog our steps? Why – dare I say it – does God seem so cruel? Why is the journey so painful and the way so hard?

Alexander Pope cynically quipped, 'Blessed is he who expects nothing, for he shall never be disappointed.' But we cannot live without hope and expectation. We have been created to love and seek fulfilment in the things that we love. Yet disappointment is inevitable, because the things we love are transient and ephemeral. We are disappointed because we fail to get what we want, but then we are disappointed when we actually do get what we want! This may be the result of foolishly naive expectations, or it may grow out of perfectly reasonable hopes that somehow came to nothing. Disappointment can be a passing emotion for a temporary loss, or it can strike at the heart of our lives and permanently hang like a shadow over us: 'always Winter but never Christmas'.[2]

But the world was never meant to be like this.

The Bible agrees. It begins with a perfect world. Life in the Garden is life in the superlative. It is life in close and intimate fellowship with God, which is the purpose of human existence. Adam and Eve walk with God in the cool of the day, and all is well.

Then, of course, comes the rebellion of Genesis chapter 3. They listen to the hiss of the serpent and entertain the idea that God is not as good as they imagined him to be. Satisfaction can be found outside of God. His word cannot be trusted, and death is a false threat. Wanting to usurp God's position, they disobey his clear command in an act of reckless independence. Death enters the world – not just physical death, but the broken relationship with God that cuts them off from the source of life itself. Like a flower cut at the stem, beauty soon fades, and death cloys their very existence.

And the world is now like a beautiful but comprehensively damaged work of art. There are still magnificent intimations of lost glory – the breathtaking sunset, that heart-warming music or the soft touch of the lover's hand. But at the same time, we are conscious that the masterpiece has been scarred with the graffiti of sin. All our joys are touched with pain.

Landscape of a broken world

The Bible paints a graphic picture of life in a broken world in the chapters that follow. Read Genesis 4 – 11 for yourself and you cannot miss it.

What are the marks of a world in rebellion against God?

Adam and Eve experience the joy of parenthood as God blesses them with two boys. The command to be fruitful, multiply and fill the earth seems to continue to have traction in their new circumstances (Genesis 1:28; 4:1–2). They acknowledge the gift of children as a sign of God's continuing grace and kindness (4:1–2). But then they lose both their sons as the elder one murders his brother and flees into a distant land. The first person born into the world after the advent of sin is a murderer, and the second a victim of extreme violence. So the first family in recorded history is deeply dysfunctional.

Can you imagine the intensity of the pain and disappointment that Eve must have felt as her heart was lacerated by sharp pangs of grief? Can you picture the bitter tears shed by Adam as the magnitude of the situation rolled over his heart in an ocean of pain? Like millions of parents afterwards, Adam and Eve must have questioned in their hearts, 'Where did we go wrong? Why didn't we see this coming?' Did they carry the scar of regret and guilt for the rest of their lives? How many nights did they wake from troubled sleep, longing for the embrace that they would never feel again?

But death has entered the bloodstream of the human race. Genesis 5 is an account of Adam's descendants all the way down to Noah. In a highly stylized way we are reminded of the certain and sure march of death:

> When Adam had lived 130 years, he had a son in his own likeness, in his own image; and he named him Seth. After Seth was born, Adam lived 800 years and had other sons and daughters.
> Altogether, Adam lived a total of 930 years, and then he died.
> (5:3–5)

Like the relentless patter of rain beating on a tin roof, the refrain is repeated seven times: '. . . and he died . . . and he died . . . and he died . . .' Human beings discover from the very beginning of recorded history that death is our constant companion. Disappointment numbs our hearts big time as death rips the people we love from our arms.

Washing the world clean

The next chapter begins with the divine assessment of the human condition:

The LORD saw how great the wickedness of the human race
had become on the earth, and that every inclination of the
thoughts of the human heart was only evil all the time.
The LORD regretted that he had made human beings on the
earth, and his heart was deeply troubled. So the LORD said,
'I will wipe from the face of the earth the human race I have
created – and with them the animals, the birds and the
creatures that move along the ground – for I regret that
I have made them.'
(Genesis 6:5–7)

The evils of the race are not a superficial skin condition that can
be healed by a soothing salve and a few bandages. The problem
is internal, a problem of the heart. Human beings have curved
in on themselves. The spring of our lives has been poisoned, and
all the waters that flow from it are contaminated. And this results
in the fearful catalogue of evil actions which prompts God to
grieve and take the monumental decision to wash the world
clean and begin all over again.

So, apart from eight souls, the entire rebellious race is swept
away. It is impossible to act decisively with human sin without
dealing judicially with the human beings who are responsible
for it. It is no wonder that the New Testament uses the story of
the flood as an archetypal picture of all of God's judgments. The
floods of God's wrath would pour down on the head of Jesus,
his Son, as he hung upon the cross (something that we will
explore later). And the final judgment of the world will one day
resemble the flood in its intensity and unavoidability (Matthew
24:37–41).

This surgical strike takes out a world in rebellion against God.
The cancer of sin has now been cut out, leaving one single family
through whom God will fulfil his purposes.

Same old problems

One single family and a fresh start. This will result in a brave new world, washed clean of all trace of evil.

Except that it doesn't.

Noah's family proves to be just as dysfunctional as Adam's. Noah gets drunk, and his son Ham sees his father's nakedness (Genesis 9:18–27). Whatever is happening here, it is clearly more than just a furtive glance, since it results in a severe word of judgment pronounced on Ham and his offspring (9:25).

The race continues and replenishes itself, and the nations are born (Genesis 10). Many of these nations will oppose God's purposes and persecute his people in the future.

This part of the divine record culminates in the misguided attempt to build a tower to reach up to heaven. It is not that God feels threatened by human ingenuity or that he despises human technology. But Genesis 11 is a kind of rerun of Genesis 3, for, like Adam and Eve, the race is seduced into thinking that it can live without reference to God. This primeval Shard is a statement of independence. Again God comes down, discovers the act of rebellion and scatters the rebels.

All this is pretty grim. Of course, there are intimations of hope in the midst of the gloom. God promises that one day he will send a serpent crusher who will defeat the devil and reverse the consequences of the curse (3:15). Enoch walks with God (5:24), and Noah finds grace with God (6:8). God hangs up his war bow and promises in solemn covenant never to destroy the world with water again (8:20–22). The rebellion and scattering at Babel are followed by the promise to Abram that God will bless the whole world through his seed (12:1–3). This covenant promise will determine the rest of history and culminate in a new heaven and a new earth.

Nonetheless, the biblical record is clear about the realities of life in the world we now inhabit.

This world now and then

If Genesis 4 – 11 is our guide, then the world we live in is a tough and inhospitable place. Gone is the peaceful satisfaction of Eden. In its place is the hostility of a fractured world. Disappointment is the breath we breathe outside the Garden. It is marked by fear and loathing, dysfunctional families and rebellious children, violence and sexual perversion, bereavement and grief, hatred of God and exploitation of humankind, anger and bitterness, betrayal and broken relationships, depression and despair and death.

And the picture painted here is just a taster of what is to come. The Bible does not pull its punches. In graphic terms, it describes this world with all its ills. Read some of the stories it contains and you might well think that there are parts of the book that are unsuitable for children. (Take a look at Genesis 38 or Judges 17 – 21 or 2 Samuel 13.)

The ultimate evidence of the true condition of the world is that when its Creator steps into history and comes to his own, they reject, despise and crucify him (John 1:10–11; Acts 2:22–23). The cross of Christ holds up a mirror before our faces and shows us the reality of our own fallen-ness. It also shows us the depths of the problem and the radical nature of the demanded solution – it takes the death and resurrection of the Son of God to repair the damage.

And therein lies the world's hope: one day Christ will purge away all the consequences of sin. He will restore all that has been lost and reunite a fractured cosmos under his wise and just reign of peace:

> In him we have redemption through his blood, the forgiveness of sins, in accordance with the riches of God's grace that he lavished on us. With all wisdom and understanding, he made known to us the mystery of his will according to his good pleasure, which he purposed in Christ, to be put into effect when the times reach

their fulfilment – to bring unity to all things in heaven and on
earth under Christ.
(Ephesians 1:7–10)

One day the results of the curse will be removed. The stain of
tears will be gone for ever and we will enjoy a perfect and
unclouded vision of God. One day death will die.

And one day my mum will recognize me again, and all that
she was previously will be restored, magnified and perfected. She
will worship the God whom she came to trust in her eighties,
and who has not deserted her even in her confusion. On that day
all things will be well.

One day disappointment will be a thing of the past, and we
will be satisfied for ever.

Trapeze anxiety

But not yet.

The resurrection of Christ guarantees the purpose of God to
make the world new and finally purge it of its sin and pain. But
that lies in the future. In the present age the whole creation groans:

> We know that the whole creation has been groaning as in the
> pains of childbirth right up to the present time. Not only so,
> but we ourselves, who have the firstfruits of the Spirit, groan
> inwardly as we wait eagerly for our adoption to sonship, the
> redemption of our bodies.
> (Romans 8:22–23)

And we groan because we are part of it. We have been adopted
into God's family and enjoy all the privileges and assurances of
sonship. But we still live in unredeemed bodies in a pain-wracked
world. We eagerly wait for resurrection morning when all the
griefs and agonies of this world will be gone for ever.

But not yet.

Have you ever watched those magnificent men and women on the flying trapeze? The 'flyer' leaves the security of the firm grip of the trapeze bar and for a fraction of a second moves through empty space with nothing between him and the ground. He is then gripped in the firm embrace of the 'catcher', who lands him safely on the cradle at the other side of the ring.

Living in a broken world is like flying through the air. We know that a new world is coming and that things will one day be different. We know for sure that Jesus will catch us. He has never dropped anyone yet. He will certainly bring God's final purposes to completion. But that does not mean that we are comfortable about traversing empty space without the presence of a safety net. For the high-wire artist, it lasts only a fraction of a second. In cosmic terms, the whole history of this poor broken world is just a brief episode in eternity. But it doesn't feel like that for us. We are creatures of time – feeble and frail – and the whole of our lives seem to exist in the unnerving space high above the ground with no visible supports. So we fly through the air with the greatest of *dis*-ease.

Being a Christian does not protect us from the thousand natural shocks that flesh is heir to. Indeed, there may be a whole series of trials that we face just *because* we are Christians and follow a crucified Saviour.

How do we respond?

We are surrounded by a cacophony of voices telling us that we should rise above negative thoughts. We should live above the fray – Christians don't allow disappointment to affect them; if we had more faith, we could escape from the prison of disappointment.

On the other side, there are friends who will encourage us to abandon our faith altogether – why bother with a God who has let you down?

The Bible is honest, and so must we be. We must frankly address those things that disappoint us. But we are supposed to do more than merely survive. In this broken world we can have real joys and solid confidences. We can enjoy the good things that God sends and find help to live grateful, fruitful lives in the midst of the surrounding brokenness.

But does God have a purpose in our disappointments? We will consider this vital question in the next chapter.

Questions

1. Read through Genesis 4 – 11. What is the evidence that we live 'outside the Garden', in a fallen world?
2. What signs of hope and grace can you find in this part of the Bible?
3. Look at a recent newspaper. What evidence can you find there that the world is broken?
4. Read Romans 8:22–23 and Ecclesiastes 12:1–8. What do they reveal about our current experience as Christians?
5. As you fly through the air, what are the things that perturb you right now? Pray that this book will equip you to invest them wisely and well.

2. The thorns remain

Charles fell in love with Maud the first time he saw her.

He was a Shropshire lad, and she was a Wiltshire girl. It was the 1940s, and he had been drafted into the RAF and then posted to Compton Bassett in north Wiltshire. He had been brought up in a strong Christian home, so one of his priorities was to find a place of worship. And that was where he set eyes upon Maud.

'She was singing in the choir and I thought she was an angel.'

They married and moved to Birmingham where, thirty years later, I married their daughter.

Charles and Maud were a wonderful example of practical godliness and marital devotion. She was always his 'girlie', and he wrote her a poem on every wedding anniversary. Their children may have made fun of the doggerel, but they rejoiced in the constancy that this love displayed.

In later years trials came, including the death of Lizzie, their eldest daughter. Maud suffered from diabetes and intense pain. After a series of unsuccessful operations, they had to amputate first one leg and then the other. Then phantom pains set in.

Sitting with her one afternoon, I asked about her favourite hymns. They were old-school, and I recognized most of her choices, but there was one that we had to look up:

> My God, I thank thee, who hast made
> The earth so bright;
> So full of splendour and of joy,
> Beauty and light;
> So many glorious things are here,
> Noble and right.[1]

As Christians, we should rejoice in all God's good gifts and receive them with thanksgiving: 'Every good and perfect gift is from above, coming down from the Father of the heavenly lights, who does not change like shifting shadows' (James 1:17).

This, of course, includes a world 'full of splendour and of joy, beauty and light'. The hymn goes on to affirm that even

> in the darkest spot of earth
> Some love is found.

When we look at a glorious panorama of God's creation, or dangle our children on our knees, or sit down to a delicious meal prepared by loving hands, we are supposed to look up with gratitude to the God who has so generously given us all these things. It is blasphemous to think of him as parsimonious or tight-fisted. The tokens of his goodness are all around us. He is open-handed and bounteous in all that he does. Indeed, he is the one who 'richly provides us with everything for our enjoyment' (1 Timothy 6:17). And these gifts are given to all people, irrespective of their relationship with God. Theologians call it God's 'common grace' – his uncommon goodness to all he has made.

The battle for our hearts

But here is the problem. Mum's hymn goes on to say,

> I thank thee, too, that all our joy
> Is touched with pain,
> That shadows fall on brightest hours,
> That thorns remain;
> So that earth's bliss may be our guide,
> And not our chain.

So often the human heart turns the gift into the ultimate good and forgets the Giver entirely. In the apostle Paul's words, we worship the creature rather than the Creator (Romans 1:25). This is the essence of idolatry. The human heart loves to make idols of the good things God gives us (Ezekiel 14:3). 'Man's nature is a perpetual factory of idols,' says John Calvin.[2]

And Martin Luther gets to the heart of the matter when he says,

> A god is that to which we look for all good and in which we find refuge in every time of need. The trust and faith of the heart . . . make both God and idol . . . That to which your heart clings and entrusts itself is really your God.[3]

What do you dream about? Where do you run for refuge? What do you delight in? What do you esteem, love, trust, fear and desire? Idols are the things that we treasure. They can be anything that hinders us from loving God supremely and anything that rivals Jesus in our affections. Idolatry occurs when we turn good things into ultimate things.

Here's what Tim Keller says:

> Sin isn't only doing bad things, it is more fundamentally making good things into ultimate things. Sin is building your life and

meaning on anything, even a very good thing, more than on God. Whatever we build our life on will drive us and enslave us. Sin is primarily idolatry.[4]

And this is the reason why all our joy is touched with pain. It is why God sets a shadow on the brightest moments in our lives. He allows the thorns to remain:

> So that earth's bliss may be our guide,
> And not our chain.

We can indeed enjoy what God has generously given – it would be a mark of ingratitude and rudeness to do otherwise. But these things should lead us upwards and onwards, guiding us to God, so that we kiss the hand that gives them. But at the same time, they are always tinged with disappointment so that they cannot anchor us to earth like a great 'chain'.

God is so good that we can refer to his good gifts as tokens of bliss. Yet it is easy to shift our focus away from him even as we unwrap the gift. Disappointment is a blessing, simply because it keeps us grounded.

It's high time we defined disappointment.

What exactly is disappointment?

Disappointment is the sadness experienced when people or circumstances do not fulfil our expectations. It occurs when there is a disparity between expectation and experience – between hope and outcome. We look to something to give us satisfaction or significance and, having reached our desired goal, discover that the desired result has not been achieved. The greater the expectation, the greater the disappointment. This can apply to small and comparatively insignificant things: a less-than-perfect holiday, an unexpected exit in the third round of the FA cup or an overpriced but bland meal. Or it can encompass huge life-changing moments: a failed marriage, a chronic illness or an agonizing bereavement.

Suddenly I discover that life is not what I hoped it would be. I well remember the sting of pain when they told me that my dad would not survive his cancer. The anticipation of joyfully presenting him with numerous grandchildren evaporated in a single moment. Disappointment is associated with the feeling of what might have been compared to what exists in the present. I don't have, I didn't get, and I will never achieve what I anticipated.

It must be said, though, that some people seem to take the most horrendous disappointments in their stride and recover quickly. Others get mired in frustration, blame, depression and bitterness. We might become angry with a parent, a spouse, an employer or a friend. We may even become angry with God. Sometimes we will not accept the situation and continue to dream of the idealized object of satisfaction. This may be a healthy spur to further action, or it might become a pathological retreat from the realities of life. It may seem easier to get angry than to live with disappointment – but it is always unhelpful in the long run. Other common reactions are apathy: 'Why bother about anything?', or guilt: 'I must have done something wrong', and low self-esteem: 'This is further proof that I am not worth much.'

And disappointment is universal. Ambrose Bierce defined a year as a 'period of three hundred and sixty-five disappointments'.[5] In the much loved children's classic, *Anne of Green Gables*, Anne rather histrionically laments,

> Well, that is another hope gone. 'My life is a perfect graveyard of buried hopes.' That's a sentence I read in a book once, and I say it over to comfort myself whenever I'm disappointed in anything.[6]

In recent years a whole 'psychology of disappointment' has even emerged. Perhaps it is related to the fact that material prosperity and comparative comfort in our culture raise expectations and give us a sense of entitlement that can never be fully satisfied. It is well known that millennials have issues in this area, often triggered by social media.

Sad saints – and sinners

If disappointment is indeed 'the sadness experienced when people or circumstances do not fulfil our expectations', then the Bible is full of examples.

Naomi is devastated at the loss of her husband and sons (Ruth 1:20). Hannah is aggrieved at her childlessness (1 Samuel 1:10). Samuel mourns the failure and rejection of Saul (1 Samuel 15:11). Elijah's hope almost collapses when he sees the apparent invincibility of evil (1 Kings 19:4). Paul is shocked that the Galatian Christians can so quickly abandon the gospel (Galatians 1:6).

The prophet Jeremiah laments over the disappointment of shattered hopes:

> We hoped for peace
>   but no good has come,
> for a time of healing
>   but there is only terror.
> (Jeremiah 8:15)

Wisdom tells us that

> Hope deferred makes the heart sick,
>   but a longing fulfilled is a tree of life.
> (Proverbs 13:12)

Sometimes disappointment is the result of sin. When Ahab cannot get Naboth's vineyard, his disappointment leads to a petulant display of self-pity: 'So Ahab went home, sullen and angry because Naboth the Jezreelite had said, "I will not give you the inheritance of my ancestors." He lay on his bed sulking and refused to eat' (1 Kings 21:4).

His manipulative wife, Jezebel, uses this self-indulgence to steer him towards murder (1 Kings 21:5–16). Eventually, he achieves his desired goal, but at what cost! Uncontrolled disappointment can indeed be incredibly dangerous.

On other occasions God uses disappointment to alert his people to the fact that their priorities are not as they should be. Haggai prophesied to the exiles who had returned from Babylon. Instead of building the temple, they had concentrated on their own comforts. But their harvests had been disappointing:

> 'You expected much, but see, it turned out to be little. What you brought home, I blew away. Why?' declares the LORD Almighty. 'Because of my house, which remains a ruin, while each of you is busy with your own house. Therefore, because of you the heavens have withheld their dew and the earth its crops. I called for a drought on the fields and the mountains, on the grain, the new wine, the olive oil and everything else the ground produces, on people and livestock, and on all the labour of your hands.'
> (Haggai 1:9–11)

After the crucifixion the disciples collapsed into an abyss of disappointment because they had failed to understand God's purposes at the cross:

> He was a prophet, powerful in word and deed before God and all the people. The chief priests and our rulers handed him over to be sentenced to death, and they crucified him; but we had hoped that he was the one who was going to redeem Israel. And what is more, it is the third day since all this took place. In addition, some of our women amazed us. They went to the tomb early this morning but didn't find his body. They came and told us that they had seen a vision of angels, who said he was alive. Then some of

our companions went to the tomb and found it just as the women
had said, but they did not see Jesus.
(Luke 24:19–24)

A disappointed God?

Here's a thought: can God be disappointed? The verses we saw
in chapter 1 seem to suggest that he can indeed be:

> The LORD saw how great the wickedness of the human race had
> become on the earth, and that every inclination of the thoughts of
> the human heart was only evil all the time. The LORD regretted that
> he had made human beings on the earth, and his heart was deeply
> troubled. So the LORD said, 'I will wipe from the face of the earth
> the human race I have created – and with them the animals, the birds
> and the creatures that move along the ground – for I regret that I
> have made them.' But Noah found favour in the eyes of the LORD.
> (Genesis 6:5–8)

Later we read that God was grieved by Israel's constant rebellion:

> How often they rebelled against him in the wilderness
>   and grieved him in the wasteland!
> (Psalm 78:40)

> Yet they rebelled
>   and grieved his Holy Spirit.
> So he turned and became their enemy
>   and he himself fought against them.
> (Isaiah 63:10)

This anticipates the references to the grieving of the Holy
Spirit – the third Person of the Trinity – in the New Testament
(Ephesians 4:30).

It is the idolatry of the people that has particularly grieved God's heart:

> Then in the nations where they have been carried captive, those who escape will remember me – how I have been grieved by their adulterous hearts, which have turned away from me, and by their eyes, which have lusted after their idols. They will loathe themselves for the evil they have done and for all their detestable practices.
> (Ezekiel 6:9)

All of these examples certainly sound like disappointment. They cannot mean that God is fickle, driven by passing emotions. Neither can they mean that he is somehow taken by surprise and shocked by something he never anticipated. However, they do refer to a reality within the divine heart. God's responses are vastly different from our unreliable and unstable emotions. They flow from a perfect and unchangeable character. They are, nonetheless, true and authentic responses which have some analogy in our human experience.

A disappointed Saviour

When we turn to Jesus, we are on surer ground. It is very clear that, as a human being, Jesus did in fact experience disappointment. After returning from his Transfiguration, he discovered that his disciples had failed to help a demonized boy and he responds to the situation with evident frustration: 'You unbelieving and perverse generation . . . how long shall I stay with you and put up with you?' (Luke 9:41).

In the shortest verse in the Bible John tells us that 'Jesus wept' (John 11:35). Here is the Son of God expressing his sorrow and anger in the face of death. Here is a Saviour who knows and feels our sorrows.

As he approaches Jerusalem, aware that in less than a week the city will reject him and demand his crucifixion, he weeps over the city and laments,

> If you, even you, had only known on this day what would bring you peace – but now it is hidden from your eyes. The days will come upon you when your enemies will build an embankment against you and encircle you and hem you in on every side. They will dash you to the ground, you and the children within your walls. They will not leave one stone on another, because you did not recognise the time of God's coming to you.
> (Luke 19:42–44)

Under the shadow of the cross Jesus goes to Gethsemane. In this, the moment of his greatest distress, he looks to his disciples for support. But instead, he finds them sleeping: ' "Simon," he said to Peter, "are you asleep? Couldn't you keep watch for one hour? Watch and pray so that you will not fall into temptation. The spirit is willing, but the flesh is weak" ' (Mark 14:37–38).

Like us, Jesus knew the reality of disappointment.

But, dare we ask, was he ever disappointed with God, his Father?

Think of his striking words from the cross: 'About three in the afternoon Jesus cried out in a loud voice, *"Eli, Eli, lema sabachthani?"* (which means "My God, my God, why have you forsaken me?")' (Matthew 27:46; Mark 15:34).

These words express both anguish and trust.

There is the deep and dreadful anguish of divine desertion. In some inexplicable way, the Father, who has always been so close to him, turns away his smiling face and plunges the sword of divine judgment into the bosom of his own Son. Here is suffering beyond anything we can ever imagine.

At the same time the words are a quotation from Psalm 22. This psalm expresses pain, but it also anticipates victory:

I will declare your name to my people;
in the assembly I will praise you.
You who fear the LORD, praise him!
All you descendants of Jacob, honour him!
Revere him, all you descendants of Israel!
For he has not despised or scorned
the suffering of the afflicted one;
he has not hidden his face from him
but has listened to his cry for help.
(Psalm 22:22–24)

Jesus was not taken by surprise – he knew the anguish that he would face at the cross. He was not disappointed in God – he expresses a sure and certain confidence in him. The pain does not destroy his trust.

What does all this mean for us? If Jesus is the perfect example of true humanity, we can be certain that disappointment is not alien to human experience. We should not be surprised when it happens. Equally, we find assurance here that disappointment is not necessarily sinful. Sometimes it can be a godly response to the hardness of the human heart or the pain of a broken world. It should also encourage us to remember that Jesus is our High Priest who is able to sympathize with us in our weaknesses because he was tempted like us in every way (Hebrews 4:15).

There is a purpose in disappointment. And the greatest purpose of all is to drive us into the arms of Jesus.

Mum's hymn goes on to hold out this wonderful solution:

I thank thee, Lord, that here our souls,
Though amply blest,
Can never find, although they seek,
A perfect rest,
Nor ever shall, until they lean
On Jesus' breast.

Maud and Charles went to be with Jesus many years ago now, but when I shut my eyes, I can still picture that conversation on a warm spring afternoon. I was still in my twenties. My wife was pregnant with our firstborn, and life seemed to be full of thorn-free roses. The miscarriage radically changed our perceptions. Decades of pastoral ministry have only confirmed what I learned that afternoon. The world is broken, and disappointment is inevitable.

So disappointment is common to all human experience – but if I am a Christian, am I really allowed to feel like this? Let's find out.

Questions

1. James 1:17 tells us that all good and perfect gifts come from the hand of God. What does this teach us about God?
2. Charles Spurgeon once said, 'We write our blessings in the sand and carve our complaints in marble.' What does this show about human nature?
3. What gifts has God given to you? Why do we constantly turn our affection from the Giver to the gifts?
4. Disappointment is 'the sadness experienced when people or circumstances do not fulfil our expectations'. Is this a good definition of disappointment? How might it be improved?
5. 'Hope deferred makes the heart sick' (Proverbs 13:12). What does this teach us about disappointment?
6. How does the fact that Jesus experienced disappointment help us when we are disappointed? Apply this to your own situation today and invest wisely.

3. Am I allowed to feel like this?

I met my first articulate atheist when I was sixteen.

Mr Hughes was my English teacher. He inspired me to love Chaucer and Shakespeare and John Donne. But his greatest achievement was to give me a lifelong love for the poetry of T. S. Eliot. Under his expert tutelage we negotiated a tortuous path through *The Waste Land*. In this poem Eliot describes the malaise of Western society which has lost its spiritual bearings and is absorbed in materialism and hedonism. It is a picture of a world that is morally bankrupt and spiritually adrift:

> Unreal City,
> Under the brown fog of a winter dawn,
> A crowd flowed over London Bridge, so many,
> I had not thought death had undone so many.[1]

In class we debated the nature of life and the possible existence of a higher power and a greater purpose. Mr Hughes was convinced that life was raw and ragged and ultimately pointless. More than once he told us in his beautifully lilting Welsh accent,

Life is like a string of pearls. As you grow older, you will
see that it is threaded with one disappointment after another.
Get used to it. You will come to understand, boys, that life
is one long period of despair, punctuated by lighter moments
of depression, but ending in the dreadful futility of the
grave.

As you can imagine, English lessons were a laugh a minute!

But Mr Hughes was not mean with his atheism. He knew
that I was a Christian and not once did he belittle me or make
fun of my faith. His view of life was more that of the weary
traveller who has been on a difficult and painful journey and
concluded that there is no guide to show the way and nothing
at the end of it to bring solace and comfort. His atheism was
not the logical conclusion of a carefully worked-out argu-
ment, but rather the result of looking at a world so full
of heartache and sorrow and reaching the painful conclusion
that there is no room for a loving God with a wise and good
purpose.

If he ever said anything critical about Christians, it was that
they did not take the pain of life seriously enough. His perception
was that they were simplistic about the complexities of life. They
used their faith as a kind of shield that prevented them from
experiencing pain, disappointment and disillusionment. They
opted to live in a cloud cuckoo land where faith meant not asking
the difficult questions. The power of positive thinking would
prevail and clear away all the mists of disappointment that might
cloud our horizons.

Was he right about Christians?

As a Christian, am I allowed to ask questions? When disappointment floods my life, is it OK to be despondent and
confused? Am I really allowed to feel like this?

We will turn to Ecclesiastes, a book that tackles the
disappointments of life head-on.

Doing life well

There are three books in the Bible that explore the themes of doing life well: Proverbs, Ecclesiastes and Job. Together, they are referred to as the wisdom literature. They seek to answer questions such as: 'What does it mean to live well in this world?' and 'How can I live a good, purposeful and significant life?'

To get at the answer, we must listen to all three voices.

In the book of Proverbs we hear the voice of Wisdom, personified as an astute and gracious lady who wants to direct us in her ways. She offers her insights to everyone who will listen. Wisdom is relational and not merely intellectual. It begins with a right relationship with God:

> The fear of the LORD is the beginning of knowledge,
>   but fools despise wisdom and instruction.
> (Proverbs 1:7)

Many of the proverbs are neat and tidy aphorisms or general statements which affirm that in most circumstances the world makes sense: wise people do wise things and they prosper; foolish people do foolish things and they pay for it. If we live in a wise way, we will flourish; if we live in a foolish way, we will crash and burn. This should not surprise us, because we live in a moral universe in which God is not an absentee landlord. There are principles at work in the world that make sense. If you work hard and plan carefully, your business will succeed. But if you are slothful and imprudent, it will fail. If you invest time in your children and do not neglect them, they will do well. If you fail to do these things, don't be surprised when they go astray. Prudence is good; impulsiveness is bad.

This is the world of the Proverbs. Wise people do well in life and are free from disappointments. They live lives that are healthy, prosperous, long and rich. Fear God and you will live a long and prosperous life.

This is how life works. Except that sometimes it doesn't!

Sometimes, it has to be said, hard work does not pay off. Sometimes we fear God, but our children still go off the rails. Sometimes doing the wise thing gets us into trouble. If the Proverbs are treated as a series of promises of assured and desirable results that we can trust with cast-iron certainty, then we will find that life does not work like that. Our expectations are not realized. Hopes are dashed. We are heading for disappointment.

To get the full picture, however, we must listen to two other voices: those of Job and Ecclesiastes.

An antidote to the power of positive thinking

The ancient book of Job has been a comfort to Christians for centuries. It begins with an open secret. Three times we are told that Job was 'blameless and upright', that 'he feared God and shunned evil' (1:1, 8; 2:3). It is clear from the start that his suffering is not the result of any secret and unconscious sin on his part. Here is a good guy. And yet he loses his possessions, his children and his health (Job 1:13–19; 2:6–8).

How does he respond?

> The LORD gave and the LORD has taken away;
>   may the name of the LORD be praised.
> (1:21)

Later Job will confess his confusion, but even as he does so, there are moments when his faith seems to rise above his circumstances. He may complain to God, but he will not surrender his faith (13:15). He believes that his suffering is purposeful and will come to an end:

> But he knows the way that I take;
>   when he has tested me, I shall come forth as gold.
> (23:10)

It is this vacillating between hope and despair that confirms the authenticity of the book and makes it so 'real' and so helpful. Isn't this exactly our experience too when we are disappointed?

At the end of the book Job meets with God and comes to submit to his sovereignty and wisdom (42:1–6). He is reconciled to God, and his prosperity is restored.

The book of Job reminds us of the overwhelming mysteries of life and the magnitude of suffering which sometimes overtakes us. Job teaches us that sometimes good people do suffer. Yet God has not deserted them – indeed, God is in control of all the circumstances of our lives, even when they seem absolutely dire. Think of the cross, where the most innocent man ever experienced ultimate suffering. We must trust God's hand even when we cannot trace his heart, difficult though this may be.

I have dealt with Job in an earlier book if you would like to explore this further.[2]

Preacher in the laboratory

Ecclesiastes is a God-given antidote to a simplistic reading of the book of Proverbs. Things don't always work out as we expect. The challenges of the book reflect the very real challenges of real life.

Listen to the opening words:

> It is useless, useless, said the Philosopher. Life is useless, all useless. You spend your life working, labouring, and what do you have to show for it? Generations come and generations go, but the world stays just the same.
> (Ecclesiastes 1:2–4 GNT)

The author identifies himself as 'Koheleth' or the 'Preacher'. He is an experienced man who is sharp in his observations and perceptive in his insights. He has engaged with life in the fullest sense of the word and he wants us to share the fruits of his experience. He has treated life as a kind of laboratory in which he has experimented to discover what brings ultimate satisfaction. What can we experience in the transience of life that will not end in disappointment and disillusionment?

He tried pleasure:

I denied myself nothing my eyes desired;
    I refused my heart no pleasure.
My heart took delight in all my labour,
    and this was the reward for all my toil.
Yet when I surveyed all that my hands had done
    and what I had toiled to achieve,
everything was meaningless, a chasing after the wind;
    nothing was gained under the sun.
(2:10–11)

Then he turned to wisdom or education – labs, libraries and lecture halls:

I saw that wisdom is better than folly,
    just as light is better than darkness.
The wise have eyes in their heads,
    while the fool walks in the darkness;
but I came to realise
    that the same fate overtakes them both.
(2:13–14)

The end of the wise and the foolish is the same: wisdom does not prolong life or bring satisfaction.

The same is true of toil:

So my heart began to despair over all my toilsome labour under the sun. For a person may labour with wisdom, knowledge and skill, and then they must leave all they own to another who has not toiled for it. This too is meaningless and a great misfortune. What do people get for all the toil and anxious striving with which they labour under the sun? All their days their work is grief and pain; even at night their minds do not rest. This too is meaningless.

(2:20–23)

Every experiment ended in disappointment.

Life is disturbing

As the Preacher looks at life, he finds it to be profoundly disturbing. Three things trouble him.

First, he is struck by the inevitable march of time. Human life is fleeting:

> What do people gain from all their labours
>   at which they toil under the sun?
> Generations come and generations go,
>   but the earth remains for ever.
> The sun rises and the sun sets,
>   and hurries back to where it rises.
>
> (1:3–5)

We are just a blip in time. Generations come and go, but the world has been here long before us and will continue long after we are gone. No-one remembers people from long ago, and the people to come will be forgotten. Blink and life is gone!

Old age never comes alone, so remember God before it is too late:

> Remember him – before the silver cord is severed,
>   and the golden bowl is broken;

before the pitcher is shattered at the spring,
   and the wheel broken at the well,
and the dust returns to the ground it came from,
   and the spirit returns to God who gave it.
(12:6–7)

It is all very well using euphemisms – we are 'chronologically gifted' rather than just plain old – but this does not mask the grim realities: 'Sans teeth, sans eyes, sans taste, sans everything'.[3]

That leads the Preacher naturally to the second thing that troubles him: the universal reality of death:

For the wise, like the fool, will not be long remembered;
   the days have already come when both have been forgotten.
Like the fool, the wise too must die!
(2:16)

Humans face the same destiny as dumb creatures. It does not matter whether you are good or bad, wise or foolish – the same fate awaits us all. That is why it is

better to go to a house of mourning
   than to go to a house of feasting,
for death is the destiny of everyone;
   the living should take this to heart.
(7:2)

Third, the Preacher is troubled by the fact that life seems so random. The rigid cause and effect observed in Proverbs just does not always hold true. There is a bug in the system. Life malfunctions. Anomalies occur:

I have seen something else under the sun:

The race is not to the swift
   or the battle to the strong,

nor does food come to the wise
  or wealth to the brilliant
  or favour to the learned;
but time and chance happen to them all.
(9:11)

You cannot control the future. If you think that playing by the rules always results in a beneficial outcome, think again. Remember Job!

I think that Mr Hughes would have approved of the Preacher's take on life!

Smoke gets in your eyes

To engage with these alarming observations, the Preacher uses two phrases.

His favourite description of life is that it is *hebel*. This Hebrew word, used thirty-eight times, is usually translated 'meaningless' or 'vanity'. It is a mixture of frustration, regret and disappointment. Life is like a breath on the breeze. We try to grasp it and it is gone. It is like a bubble of soapy water – for a moment it is caught in a sunbeam and it appears translucent in its beauty, but touch it and it evaporates. Life is beautiful, perplexing, bewildering and uncontrollable.

He appears to give an alternative view on life to that articulated in other parts of the Bible. This has led some people to dismiss its author as an agnostic, or even an atheist, who has somehow smuggled an alien theology under the radar of biblical orthodoxy. He sounds more like Richard Dawkins than the apostle Paul.

But this is a serious misunderstanding of both the content and purpose of this book.

Next to 'meaningless', the second common phrase is 'under the sun', which occurs twenty-eight times. It is a coded way of speaking about life on earth bounded by time and space:

I have seen all the things that are done under the sun; all of them are meaningless, a chasing after the wind.

What is crooked cannot be straightened;
    what is lacking cannot be counted.
(1:14–15)

Take God out of the picture, and what do you find? A world that is crooked and unjust and unfair.

Digging deeper

Some commentators take Ecclesiastes to be semi-autobiographical, telling the life story of Solomon. At the start of his life Solomon enjoyed an intimate relationship with God, marked by the fear of the Lord and the wisdom that flows from this (1 Kings 3:1–15). But in latter days he turned to folly and replaced the knowledge of God with a love for his many wives and their idols. Ecclesiastes describes the emptiness of a life without God. It contains the painful reflections of a man who has fallen away from his faith and is now desperately trying to fill life with anything other than God. He turns the good gifts of God into the ultimate prizes and ends up utterly disillusioned and dissatisfied.

There is certainly some traction in this view, and it works quite well for the first few chapters. But the latter chapters do not really fit this mould.

The kinds of questions and doubts raised in this book are common to many mature Christians. A few seem to sail through life unfazed by doubt and untroubled by confusion. But sooner or later most of us will experience the kind of questions posed by the Preacher. We have stood in the laboratory of life long enough to experience the fact that truth is not always recognized and injustice dogs the steps of just people.

The Preacher is describing life under the sun. This is not the experience of someone who has abandoned God. It is the common experience of all human beings as they struggle with life and all its disappointments. Christians are not immune. Indeed, in some ways their belief in a just God who directs the affairs of humankind makes the problem even more acute.

We go through times when we are confident that God is at work for good in our lives. But then there are others when things just do not make sense. The wrong people suffer; pain is excessive; justice does not prevail; life is unfair. Disappointments meet us at every corner. Like the Preacher, we feel our infirmity and fragility, and we don't have a ready answer.

So how do we gain our footing?

Ecclesiastes points us in two directions.

Enjoy what God sends

First, the Preacher advises us that since we cannot control life, we should stop trying! Enjoy what God has given you while you have it, but hold it with an open hand:

> A person can do nothing better than to eat and drink and find satisfaction in their own toil. This too, I see, is from the hand of God, for without him, who can eat or find enjoyment? (2:24–25)

and again:

> Go, eat your food with gladness, and drink your wine with a joyful heart, for God has already approved what you do. Always be clothed in white, and always anoint your head with oil. Enjoy life with your wife, whom you love, all the days of this meaningless life that God has given you under the sun – all your meaningless days. For this is your lot in life and in your toilsome

labour under the sun. Whatever your hand finds to do, do it with all your might, for in the realm of the dead, where you are going, there is neither working nor planning nor knowledge nor wisdom.

(9:7–10; see also 3:12–13, 22)

We cannot control what happens to us – but we can control how we respond. And one response is to receive with gratitude all God's good gifts. Enjoy a meal with friends; find satisfaction at the end of a good day's work; relish those times you can spend with the people you love. Make the most of every opportunity.

One of the temptations that disappointment brings is to try to cut the connection between expectation and satisfaction. If you expect nothing, you will never be disappointed. In a subtle and pernicious way this can lead to a kind of non-Christian other-worldly asceticism which refuses all God's gifts. Don't enjoy it, because you will one day lose it. It is possible to go through life without engaging and getting hurt. Ecclesiastes will have nothing of this. God 'richly provides us with everything for our enjoyment' (1 Timothy 6:17). It is an act of ingratitude, as we saw earlier, to refuse to accept his good gifts.

The last word

The second help the Preacher gives us is to remind us that although we may not be able to understand it, life does have a meaning. What we do now does have consequences. So enjoy life while you are young, but remember that a day of reckoning is coming:

You who are young, be happy while you are young,
    and let your heart give you joy in the days of your youth.
Follow the ways of your heart
    and whatever your eyes see,

but know that for all these things
> God will bring you into judgment.
So then, banish anxiety from your heart
> and cast off the troubles of your body,
> for youth and vigour are meaningless.
(11:9–10)

Learn wisdom and live in fear of the Lord. It may not guarantee success here, but it is the right thing to do. Fear God and obey his commandments. He does not want to make you lose hope; he wants to make you humble. Trust that life has meaning even when you cannot make sense of it. One day God will bring his justice on all we have done:

Now all has been heard;
> here is the conclusion of the matter:
fear God and keep his commandments,
> for this is the duty of all mankind.
For God will bring every deed into judgment,
> including every hidden thing,
> whether it is good or evil.
(12:13–14)

Christians should be neither simplistic nor naive about the confusion and disappointments of this life. The book of Ecclesiastes helps us in all sorts of ways when we wrestle with these things. It gives us permission to ask questions such as: 'Am I allowed to feel like this?'

Ecclesiastes stands at our shoulder and assures us that such feelings are indeed normal. Yes, I am allowed to feel like this.

We are now embarking on our journey through the Land of Disappointment. In the next six chapters we will consider the landscape of this familiar terrain.

Questions

1. Christians sometimes use their faith as 'a kind of shield that prevents them from experiencing pain, disappointment and disillusionment'. How is this a misuse of faith?
2. Why do we feel guilty when we have doubts?
3. Why is it dangerous to suppress our doubts? What are the consequences if we do so?
4. How do we enjoy God's gifts without allowing them to control us? What does it mean to hold them lightly?
5. Read the first and the last chapters of Ecclesiastes. What do you learn about life here?

Travelling through the
Land of Disappointment

4. 'Only seventeen years to go': when work frustrates us

As a teenager, I did several jobs, but one in particular sticks in my mind.

I had just finished my first year at university. They gave you grants to study in those days, and you did not have to pay student fees. Can you imagine! However, my parents struggled to make ends meet, so I was pleased to get a job for three months during the summer vacation. I worked in an education college in the leafy suburb of the Bourneville district of Birmingham. It sounds very grand, but I was actually in the kitchen washing the dishes. I had two shifts: 6 a.m. until 10 a.m. and 4 p.m. until 8 p.m. It suited me perfectly. I visited Edrie during her lunch hour, and for the rest of the time I worked hard on New Testament Greek.

Naturally, I got to know a few of my fellow workers. Derek was a proud Brummie in his forties. He had a permanent job in the kitchen and his shifts were slightly more sociable than mine, but we overlapped a bit. During our coffee breaks we would get to chat. He told me that he had left school at sixteen and had done several jobs, but he had been here in Bourneville for the past twenty years. He intended staying until retirement. 'Only seventeen years to go and then I can really enjoy life,' he said.

Enjoying life, for Derek, meant watching Aston Villa Football Club, going fishing and an annual trip to Blackpool. Retirement meant even more of the same.

I don't know whether or not he made it.

I never did have the courage to ask Derek if he felt fulfilled in his job. But it would have driven me nuts. I survived because it was temporary. As I said, I saw Edrie every lunchtime, and even while I was washing dishes, my mind was elsewhere, revising Greek verbs. However, the fact that retirement dominated Derek's thinking even that far off suggested that, for him, work was a means to an end and nothing more.

Work can easily become the most frustrating and disappointing thing in our lives. Even that perfect job has its vexations. We may feel trapped. We may become bored with the repetitive routine. We may find ourselves bullied or stressed out or unappreciated. Promotion may never come, and we feel envious of our contemporaries who seem to have done so much better than we have. Phrases like 'career trajectory' and 'breaking the glass ceiling' are just a joke. Here I am, and here I will stay.

But at least there are only seventeen years to go!

Listening to the Preacher again

We will now visit a series of familiar locations on our journey through the Land of Disappointment. Let's begin with work.

We met the Preacher in the last chapter. He has much to say on this subject. Almost from the start his words address the frustrations and disappointments of work:

> What do people gain from all their labours
>   at which they toil under the sun?
> Generations come and generations go,
>   but the earth remains for ever.
> (Ecclesiastes 1:3–4)

Life is so fleeting. I am going to make an impact. My life is going to count. 'Forget it,' says the Preacher. 'You exhaust yourself with toil and then you die. The earth continues as ever, and a new generation arrives that has never heard of you.'

So how do we respond? He goes on:

> So I hated life, because the work that is done under the sun was grievous to me. All of it is meaningless, a chasing after the wind. I hated all the things I had toiled for under the sun, because I must leave them to the one who comes after me. And who knows whether that person will be wise or foolish? Yet they will have control over all the fruit of my toil into which I have poured my effort and skill under the sun. This too is meaningless. So my heart began to despair over all my toilsome labour under the sun. For a person may labour with wisdom, knowledge and skill, and then they must leave all they own to another who has not toiled for it. This too is meaningless and a great misfortune. What do people get for all the toil and anxious striving with which they labour under the sun? All their days their work is grief and pain; even at night their minds do not rest. This too is meaningless.
>
> (2:17–23)

Clearly, his work was important to him. He worked with 'wisdom, knowledge and skill', pouring out his life in 'anxious striving' and 'toilsome labour'. He wanted to do the best he could. But when he stood back, he became convinced that it was all a waste of energy. Once he has gone, no-one will appreciate the labour of his hands. Days of painful toil and nights of disturbed sleep are for nothing. No-one will even say thank you. Once the gold watch is in your pocket, they will be glad to see the back of you. This makes work grievous and frustrating.

He captures the reality of this in a poignant little parable later in the book:

> There was once a small city with only a few people in it. And a
> powerful king came against it, surrounded it and built huge siege
> works against it. Now there lived in that city a man poor but wise,
> and he saved the city by his wisdom. But nobody remembered that
> poor man. So I said, 'Wisdom is better than strength.' But the poor
> man's wisdom is despised, and his words are no longer heeded.
> (9:14–16)

So what is his solution?

> A person can do nothing better than to eat and drink and find
> satisfaction in their own toil. This too, I see, is from the hand
> of God, for without him, who can eat or find enjoyment?
> (2:24–25)

Watching 'The Villa', going fishing and looking forward to the
annual pilgrimage to Blackpool. And if you survive, in retirement
you'll really get to live!

Clearly, the Preacher is tapping into something common to
human experience. Work is frustrating when you engage in it,
and it is disappointing when others take over (see 2:21).

But is this all there is to say on the subject?

Getting our bearings

Here are three simple observations.

First, we spend more of our time working than doing anything
else, with the possible exception of sleeping. Career patterns are
changing, but most of us will still spend most of our adult years
working. One of the common complaints I often hear is that
churches neglect to give teaching or support to those whose time
is spent in the world of work. Secular employment can be
regarded as inferior to so-called full-time Christian ministry. This
is an unhealthy and unbiblical error.

Second, work is a blessing. The Bible gives us several reasons why work is important. We work to live and to support our dependants (Proverbs 31:27; 2 Thessalonians 3:12). We also work to be a blessing to others and so that we can give to those who are in need (Ephesians 4:28). It is not wrong to increase our wealth and standard of living (Proverbs 13:11). However, fine and good though these utilitarian reasons are, they do not get to the heart of why work is a blessing.

God created human beings in his own image, and part of being in his image means that we are workers, like God himself. In Genesis 1 he is the Worker-Creator whose creative plan slowly unfolds before our eyes. In Genesis 2 he calls on us to play our part in the glorious privilege of labour (Genesis 2:8, 15). From the beginning, human beings have been commissioned to guard and develop God's world.

That's where that innate, inner drive for work comes from. It also means that we want our lives to count for something. We are more than our work, but it is an important part of what we are. Jesus, standing at the carpenter's bench, demonstrates the dignity of work. Even the Preacher tells us that there is nothing better than to enjoy the work of our hands (Ecclesiastes 2:24; 3:22). When we work, we are serving God and collaborating with him, even in apparently mundane tasks. As Martin Luther put it, 'God even milks cows through you.'[1]

John Stott offers a very helpful definition: 'Work is the expenditure of energy (manual or mental or both) in the service of others, which brings fulfilment to the worker, benefit to the community and glory to God.'[2]

My third observation is that the fall has affected everything, including work. This is where the Preacher is coming from when he describes life under the sun. Humans are alienated from God, and this means that all we set our hands to is disordered by sin. The entire universe is frustrated and cries out in disappointment (Romans 8:22–23).

Adam and Eve's sin is a single act with catastrophic consequences. Everything is askew, as we saw in chapter 2. We cannot accomplish all that we imagined. At work we will experience stress, exhaustion and petty rivalry. We may feel that our gifts and abilities are overlooked and wasted. Or we might get the opportunity to exercise them, only to crash and burn afterwards. We may want to change the world, only to find ourselves disheartened by lack of any significant achievement in the end.

The secret of contentment

The apostle Paul had an important job. God had called him to be the apostle to the Gentiles. His ministry would literally change the world. However, he also experienced constant opposition and disappointments. He was hated by many of his own people, misunderstood and misrepresented by those he had served and let down by some of his fellow workers. When he wrote the letter to the Philippians, he was in a prison cell in Rome. Can you imagine his frustration? He wants to visit Spain, on the westernmost edge of the Empire. This will bring to completion the task God has given him of reaching the whole Gentile world with the gospel. Instead, all he can do is pore over maps and make plans that may never come to fruition. Here is the ultimate example of workplace frustration!

Does he share his disappointment with his readers? No. Instead, he reveals the state of his heart:

> I know what it is to be in need, and I know what it is to have plenty. I have learned the secret of being content in any and every situation, whether well fed or hungry, whether living in plenty or in want. I can do all this through him who gives me strength.
> (Philippians 4:12–13)

Paul is still passionate about his work, but it has not become an idol. His love for Christ is the thing that sustains him. Whatever frustration may come his way, he finds fulfilment in his relationship with Jesus.

How do we follow his example? Here are my suggestions:

- *Enjoy your work.* Some jobs are soul-destroying, and if we find ourselves in a place where we are constantly beaten down, then we need to seek another form of employment. However, most jobs are a mixture of good and bad. Decide to concentrate on the positive. Enjoy what you do, and don't feel embarrassed about it.
- *Don't feel guilty about career advancement.* Do as well as you can, and if there is an opportunity of advancement, don't assume that for a Christian this is a temptation rather than a God-given opportunity. Ask the right questions: 'What are my motives?' 'Will this put undue pressure on my family or my Christian service?' But never assume that promotion is always wrong.
- *Do not allow work to become your god.* Do you feel that you are indispensable? Would your office or factory or school or home collapse without you? Do you live for your work and the sense of achievement that it brings you? Work is a gift from God, but we all tend to worship the gift rather than the Giver. Guard your heart. Don't turn achievement into an idol.
- *Be prepared for frustration.* Don't be surprised when you find that even the best job has its frustrations. Most of us have to work with people, and people are difficult. They, in turn, probably find you difficult too!
- *Live a balanced life.* God made us to work – but he also made us to rest and play. There is a rhythm in life, and one of the ways of dealing with disappointment is to observe the rhythms God has woven into our lives.

- *Discover your stress busters.* What are those things that enable you to escape stress? They may include running or stamp collecting or gardening. What do you do to 'unstring your bow'? What things help you to forget pressure for a while?
- *Avoid overwork.* What makes you want to be constantly busy? How do you avoid getting stretched beyond your ability to endure? Have you learned to say 'no'?
- *Offer your work to God.* You may not feel appreciated by your boss or your co-workers or your customers. But God sees and knows all that you do, and you are working for his glory. Medieval sculptors often carved beautiful objects at the top of columns in the cathedrals and churches that they had constructed. When the building was completed, the work was invisible to the human eye. But it didn't matter because they had done it for God, and he could see it.
- *Allow frustration to drive you to God.* Like every other form of disappointment, part of its purpose is to transform us. Daily trials demand daily faith. You are allowed to pray about your work – your heavenly Father does not draw a line between the sacred and the secular. And neither should we.
- *Pray for opportunities to witness.* Christians demonstrate the difference that loving Christ can make even in the most depressing work situation. You are salt and light. You are supposed to make a difference. Be ready to 'give the reason for the hope that you have' (1 Peter 3:15) when your colleagues see the difference.
- *Look forward to the endless joy of perfect labour.* Heaven is not a glorified rest home where we will sit around all day discussing our bunions. Rather, it is a place of delight and glorious fulfilment. The Bible begins and ends with work. In the eternal state the curse with its frustration is gone, and God's servants will serve him there for ever (Revelation 22:3).

Faithful service

One last area that I need to focus on is that of Christian ministry. Some of us are involved in so-called full-time service. We work for the church or for a parachurch organization. As the doctor practises medicine, and the factory worker builds cars, and the homemaker cares for children, so some of us are engaged in the cure of souls. It's what we get paid for. All the principles above apply to those who find themselves in service of this kind. And it can prove just as frustrating, just as routine and boring, and just as prone to idolatry as any other job.

But we are all involved in ministry of some sort. Those who are redeemed are recruited. Every Christian has at least one God-given gift that is to be used for the glory of God and the good of the church. And there are particular challenges when it comes to Christian service. When I cut the lawn, I can smell the cut grass. When I washed dishes in my long-ago holiday job, I could see the way they sparkled in the sunlight. When I was a teacher, end-of-term exams measured how successfully I had taught my pupils. But how exactly do you evaluate spiritual fruit? How do you measure the invisible?

You may look at numbers, but they can be misleading. The praise of your peers can be equally deceptive. So what constitutes success in ministry? What does it look like?

In the end, what matters is pleasing God, and what pleases him is faithfulness: 'This, then, is how you ought to regard us: as servants of Christ and as those entrusted with the mysteries God has revealed. Now it is required that those who have been given a trust must prove faithful' (1 Corinthians 4:1–2).

This is not an excuse for inactivity, but a call for bold action and courageous faith. Faith trusts God and then takes risks. Think of the examples in Hebrews 11. All these men and women had two things in common.

First, they acted boldly and did great things for God: Noah built a boat; Abraham left everything he knew to follow God;

Moses sacrificed the comforts of Egypt for the disgrace of identifying with a despised and hated people (Hebrews 11:7, 8–9, 24–26). There was nothing passive about their faithfulness.

Second, they did not get to experience the fullness of the promises that God made to them: 'These were all commended for their faith, yet none of them received what had been promised, since God had planned something better for us so that only together with us would they be made perfect' (Hebrews 11:39–40).

In ministry I do the best I can with the resources that God has given me and with the passion that my love for Christ inspires. Then I leave the results to God. Mine is the faithfulness; his is the fruitfulness.

Jesus teaches this in one of his most delightful parables:

> This is what the kingdom of God is like. A man scatters seed on the ground. Night and day, whether he sleeps or gets up, the seed sprouts and grows, though he does not know how. All by itself the soil produces corn – first the stalk, then the ear, then the full grain in the ear. As soon as the corn is ripe, he puts the sickle to it, because the harvest has come.
> (Mark 4:26–29)

My responsibility is to sow the seed and watch for the harvest. Everything in between is down to God. What goes on under the surface of the ground is invisible. It would be a mistake to keep on digging up the roots to inspect them. We cannot always see what God is doing, but we know that he is active. Only on the last day will we see what he has done with the seed that we sowed.

So don't be disappointed. Get on with what he asks you to do, and leave the results to him.

Questions

1. What do you find most frustrating about your work?
2. What are the motives for work outlined above? How do these motives challenge and change the way you see your work?
3. Work through the bullet points in 'The secret of contentment' section. How are you doing in these different areas?
4. Consider John Stott's definition of work. What insights does it give to the nature and purpose of work?
5. How do we cope with the apparent lack of fruitfulness in our service for God, whether it be full-time paid service or some other form of Christian service? How would we cope with unexpected success?

5. Only people make you cry: when relationships fail

Over thirty years ago I was invited to speak at a church house party. The invitation was quite clear: 'We want you to talk about relationships.' When I asked the organizers to be more specific, they informed me that they wanted help on marriage, parenting, fellowship in the church and friendships beyond. Easy – and all this in three half-hour talks!

Well, I did my best. And they were far more appreciative than the addresses deserved. But there was one conversation that I still remember. After the talk on marriage an elderly lady caught me over coffee.

'Thank you for what you said. Young people need to hear those things.' Then, with misty eyes, she continued, 'My Dan and I were together for almost fifty years. He went to be with the Lord two years ago. There isn't a single day when I don't miss him. It's like the pulling of flesh from my bones.'

I was struck by the graphic image. What I didn't realize at the time was that she was borrowing it from John Bunyan.

Bunyan, author of *The Pilgrim's Progress*, was imprisoned in Bedford jail for unlicensed preaching. He continued to write and counsel others from his cell. His wife Elizabeth and his children visited him while he was there. He had deep affection for all of them, but he had a particular fondness for his daughter Mary who was blind. For Bunyan, the visits were bitter-sweet:

> The parting with my wife and poor children hath oft been to me in this place as the pulling the flesh from my bones . . . especially my poor blind child, who lay nearer my heart than all I had besides; O the thoughts of the hardships I thought my blind one might go under, would break my heart to pieces. Poor child, thought I, what sorrow must thou have for thy portion in this world?[1]

If you love anyone, it will cost you. Pain is the price of love. Listen to these words about grieving:

> Grief is the other side of love. It is the price paid for the ending of a precious fulfilling relationship. In fact, it is an expression of love. Everyone who loves will experience grief: as the proverb says, 'Real love will make you cry.' Grief is a universal experience, as old as the human race. Eventually each of us will die, and in the meantime, all of us will grieve.[2]

We are meant to love

We find ourselves in a whole network of relationships – family, church, friends, work and so on. And the more intimate the relationship, the more potential there is for pain. Probably the most profound instances of disappointment that we ever experience in this life are in this area. It is tempting to withdraw and hide from intimacy because we don't want to risk disappointment. If all disappointment is bad, then this would seem to be a sensible option. Don't give yourself in love to anyone. Keep your relationships formal and passion-free. Retreat into the safe citadel of your own companionship.

Doesn't this make sense? Maybe – but it is not an option if we are followers of Jesus Christ.

The Bible commands us to give ourselves away. It tells us that we are supposed to care. God cared enough to give his Son for us (John 3:16; 1 John 4:10). Jesus loved us enough to die for us (1 John 3:16). The apostles wept for those who refused to receive the gospel (Acts 20:19; Romans 9:1–3). They grieved over the failure of others (2 Corinthians 2:4–5). And they tell us that love must be sincere, devoted and costly (Romans 12:9–12).

We may be tempted to immunize ourselves against the pain of relationships, but this is to cut ourselves off from some of the most profound joys that God brings into our lives. Relationships make us human.

We will explore this area in the next three chapters.

'Not good for the man to be alone'

In Genesis 1 God creates everything out of nothing, by the power of his word, for the purpose of his glory. As he steps back, he looks at what he has done and he repeatedly declares that it is good (Genesis 1:4, 10, 12, 18, 21, 25, 31). Here is affirmation by repetition.

When we move into Genesis 2, we find that there is a single caveat to God's delight in the work of his hands. It is good, except at one point: 'The LORD God said, "It is not good for the man to be alone. I will make a helper suitable for him"' (Genesis 2:18).

To fulfil the mission of populating the earth, subduing it and ruling over it, the man needs a suitable partner (Genesis 1:28). And so God institutes the covenant of marriage. The man falls into a deep sleep, and when he wakes, he looks up into the face of the most beautiful woman he has ever seen! He does what men have been doing for centuries and bursts into poetry:

This is now bone of my bones
  and flesh of my flesh;
she shall be called 'woman,'
    for she was taken out of man.
(Genesis 2:23)

God defines marriage in specific and precise terms: 'That is why a man leaves his father and mother and is united to his wife, and they become one flesh' (Genesis 2:24).

Marriage is the lifelong covenant relationship of one man and one woman.

And therein lies much of the joy and many of the sorrows of this world. It is in this area of most personal and intimate relationship that people express the greatest pain and disappointment.

'I always thought that I would get married – why did the right person never come along?'

'After being patient for so long, why is my marriage so miserable?'

'Why isn't my husband the man I thought he was?'

'Why has my wife changed?'

'How can I live with the pain that her infidelity has caused me?'

'I want to be faithful to Jesus, but I'm only attracted to people of my own sex. Can I ever experience the same fulfilment that my straight friends talk about?'

'Becoming a Christian has put my marriage under massive strain.'

'He was everything to me. I thought we would grow old together. Now he is gone, I really don't want to go on living.'

Relationships, but . . .

As a helpful starting point, we need to be clear about holding in tension two truths:

- We can never find fulfilment or experience what it is to be truly human without deep and abiding relationships. We were never meant to go it alone.
- *We can* find this completion and fulfilment without experiencing a perfect marital relationship, or indeed any marital relationship at all.

Let us begin with the first point above.

God is relational and he has created us to be like him. The God of the Bible is unique. He is one God who has existed eternally as three persons. And these persons have an eternal and unclouded relationship of mutual love and esteem. In the Garden of Eden humans enjoyed an unblemished closeness with their Creator – they walked with him in the cool of the day. They also experienced a perfect relationship with each other, symbolized by the fact that they were naked and unashamed. The relational God has hard-wired us to feel the need to connect with other people.

Sin has disrupted this, but God's purpose in grace is to restore both the vertical and horizontal relationships for which we, as human beings, ache. Relationships are not an optional extra; they are essential to our humanity.

The Bible is full of teaching on this subject, especially in the book of Proverbs. Friends bring comfort and sympathy in times of heartache (17:17). Their commitment can supersede even the most intimate family ties (18:24). A friend tells us the truth, even when it hurts (27:5–6). As iron sharpens iron, so we are sharpened by our friends (27:17). Of course, friendships can become unhelpful, especially when they distract us from our relationship with God. And friendship, like anything else, can become an idol, taking the place of God in our affections. However, friends are one of God's most precious gifts to us.

Friendship is vital to our humanity. But this is not true of marriage. Marriages should be built on friendship, but they differ from friendship in two significant ways.

First, marriage is an exclusive covenantal relationship between one man and one woman. I should cultivate a wide range of friendships with various levels of closeness. I should not demand exclusivity from my friends, but I do demand it and give it to my marital partner. I can and should have multiple friendships, but I can only engage in one marital relationship.

Second, sexual intimacy is confined to this exclusive lifelong relationship. Sexual intercourse is one of God's most precious gifts to us. The Song of Solomon is not a sex manual, but neither is it an esoteric allegory of pure non-physical love. It is a celebration of God's good gift of sex. The marriage bed should be both honoured and enjoyed, kept pure and protected from defilement (Hebrews 13:4). God has set very clear boundaries that must not be breached.

Jesus taught that sex outside of a permanent, exclusive relationship between a man and a woman is wrong. He did not distinguish between different forms of sex outside of marriage. He therefore condemned lust (virtual sex), adultery (sex with someone who is married to another person), fornication (sex before marriage) and homosexual sex.

We live in a culture that has made sex into a defining and ultimate expression of our humanity. For many people, it has replaced God as their ultimate reference point: sex gives us a sense of self-transcendence. And yet, tragically, there seems to be a ubiquitous absence of satisfaction in the lives of so many. Read the columns of even the quality newspapers and you will find that sexual pleasure is sought with grim earnestness. Never has sex offered so much and delivered so little.

Separated from God's intended purpose in marriage, sex can never fulfil the role God intended for it. And of course, one of the lies of our society is that it is impossible to be happy without a regular and satisfying sex life. Christians sometimes buy into this. Have we forgotten that Jesus was the happiest, most fulfilled and most human person ever to exist, and that he lived and died without ever having had sex?

Singleness: a challenge and an opportunity

For many people, the most intensely disappointing life experience is the absence of a marital partner. At any one time almost a third of the adults in our community are living as single people. This is reflected in our churches. Some have never married; others have been widowed, divorced or separated. Single people react to the challenges of singleness in a whole variety of ways. For some, it is the most profound and defining issue. They cannot contemplate life without a permanent partner. For others, it is a disappointment, but they have adjusted to their situation and are very upbeat about the advantages that singleness brings. Still others are immensely grateful that they are free from the trials that marriage brings – they have chosen to be single and are content.

Most people want to be married. Married people often point out the advantages of singleness, but they will usually admit that they are glad to be married! It's easy to be glib. Many single people see their singleness as a gift, but would be very happy to exchange it for the gift of a partner with whom they could share the joys and sorrows of life.

What does the Bible say to single people?

It affirms that singleness is a gift from God. Jesus spoke of those to whom singleness was given not as a judgment but as a gift (Matthew 19:11). Singleness is not God's 'second best'. In 1 Corinthians 7:7 Paul makes a similar point. Trusting God means knowing that my current condition – single or married – is his gift for me, and I am to receive it with thanksgiving.

Single people are spared the troubles that come with marriage (1 Corinthians 7:28). Marriage is hard work. Sometimes it is a place of wonderful joy. At other times it is profoundly painful. No wonder Paul wants to spare you from this! And there is more. Single people can devote themselves fully to God's work:

I would like you to be free from concern. An unmarried man is concerned about the Lord's affairs – how he can please the Lord.

But a married man is concerned about the affairs of this world –
how he can please his wife – and his interests are divided. An
unmarried woman or virgin is concerned about the Lord's affairs:
her aim is to be devoted to the Lord in both body and spirit. But
a married woman is concerned about the affairs of this world –
how she can please her husband. I am saying this for your own
good, not to restrict you, but that you may live in a right way
in undivided devotion to the Lord.
(1 Corinthians 7:32–35)

Many Christian ministries depend on the contributions of single
people. The church has been wonderfully served by people
whose singleness gave them the time and energy to influence
the cause of Christ significantly.

This does not mean that it is easy to be single. The New Testament is positive about singleness, but marriage is still the norm.
Singles therefore have to struggle with loneliness and sexual
temptation. And often it is when we feel most alone and isolated
that we experience the most seductive temptations.

However, God does not want any of his children to be mere
survivors. He does not want us to put our lives on hold until
Mr or Miss Right finally puts in an appearance. All of us – single
or married – are to experience life in all its fullness now (John
10:10). We are to develop our relationship with God and serve
him in the church and beyond. Our goal is first to seek his
kingdom and his righteousness. Most of all, we must deal
decisively with self-pity. It is one of the worst temptations of any
form of disappointment and can paralyse us permanently. The
answer is once again to find our contentment and happiness in
the Lord.

Do not be deceived, my dear brothers and sisters. Every good gift
and perfect gift is from above, coming down from the Father of
the heavenly lights, who does not change like shifting shadows.
(James 1:16–17)

The New Testament emphasizes the importance of the church family. We are not designed to be alone. All of us, whether single or married, need to work hard at cultivating other relationships. The novelist Charlotte Brontë wrote, 'The trouble is not that I am single and likely to stay single, but that I am lonely and likely to stay lonely.'[3]

As Christians, we do not need to be alone. The church should be a place where we are part of a family (Matthew 12:48–50), where we find many brothers and sisters, fathers and mothers and children (Matthew 19:29–30).

Paul chose to live a single life and he was content with his choice. At the same time, it is obvious from Paul's letters that he felt the need for the strong support that friendship brings. As he languishes in prison waiting for execution, he writes some of the most poignant words we find in the Bible. Indeed, these may well be his last recorded statements:

> Do your best to come to me quickly, for Demas, because he loved this world, has deserted me and has gone to Thessalonica. Crescens has gone to Galatia, and Titus to Dalmatia. Only Luke is with me. Get Mark and bring him with you, because he is helpful to me in my ministry. I sent Tychicus to Ephesus. When you come, bring the cloak that I left with Carpus at Troas, and my scrolls, especially the parchments.
> (2 Timothy 4:9–13)

Can you feel his disappointment at a broken relationship? Can you grasp his longing to see his friends one more time? Can you sense his gratitude for those who have stayed faithful to the end?

Neither singleness nor marriage is permanent (Mark 12:25). One day Jesus, the bridegroom, will return for his bride. When that happens, all pain will be gone: a difficult marriage or life-changing bereavement or a divorce or unwelcome singleness. All of us should keep our focus on the moment when disappointment will be a thing of the past.[4]

Beneath the surface of marriage

So what are the challenges of marriage?

I used to run marriage preparation classes in a room that the church used as a crèche. It had a large window through which you could see the main auditorium. I would often begin by reminding the class that on Sundays they would see scores of married couples through the window. 'What do you think all these couples have in common?' I would ask. Not once did anyone come up with the answer I was looking for.

I wonder what you are thinking. The one thing they had in common was that, in every case, their marriage was the most challenging relationship that they faced. We are usually good at hiding it when we come to church, but look beneath the surface, and you will find that every blessing in marriage is graciously given and hard won.

According to Genesis 2:18, marriage was designed for both companionship and service. Husband and wife support and encourage each other as they struggle with the challenges of life in a broken world. And together they work at the God-given task of making disciples of all nations (Matthew 28:18–20).

But marriage is also a means that God uses to make us like Jesus. Marriage is hard fundamentally because we don't grasp how selfish and sinful we really are. Put two sinners in an intimate relationship where there is nowhere to hide and nowhere to run. Light the fuse and stand back! Part of the purpose of marriage is to expose our flaws and help us to grow in holiness.

Disappointment occurs when I invest heavily in any enterprise, perhaps taking a massive risk in doing so, only to discover that the outcome is not what I had expected. This is exacerbated when the pain is caused by someone I have invested in deeply and passionately. It is obvious that marriage is fertile ground for this kind of experience. No marriage can ever bear the weight of the investment that we sometimes place upon it. But it was never meant to do so.

We are profoundly flawed people, and whomever we marry will be a profoundly flawed person. If we look to them as the ultimate source of satisfaction and happiness, we will always be disappointed. In a 'bad marriage' we will experience the pain of fracture and even divorce. In a 'good marriage' we may one day come to know the devastating pain of bereavement. The secret of happiness in marriage is to make sure that you don't look to marriage for your ultimate happiness.

Michelle Graham expressed it like this:

> I looked to my husband to make me feel loved, to keep me from loneliness, to make me happy when I wasn't, to give me wise advice, to help me grow spiritually . . . the list went on. And while those things are often benefits of a healthy relationship, God did not put him in my life to fulfil my needs, otherwise I wouldn't need God anymore.[5]

A life partner is a wonderful gift, but he or she must never take the place of God. My wife is my best friend, and I don't think that I could have remained in ministry without her. But we both understand that our marriage – although lifelong – is still only temporary.

When I proposed to my wife, I took her to a windswept hill, I got down on my knees and asked her the question that she knew was coming: 'I want you to marry me, but I have to tell you that you will always be the second person in my life. God has to come first and, what is more, I think he is calling me into full-time service.'

Not the most romantic proposal ever – but at least it was honest!

'Of course, the answer is yes,' she replied, 'and I want God to be first as well.'

We have tried to build our marriage on that foundation.

Wisdom for couples

This is not a book about marriage, but here are ten pieces of advice:

- *Be grateful.* Rejoice in the partner God has given you. Thank him every day for his grace and kindness in putting this person in your life.
- *Guard your heart.* Don't allow your marriage to become an idol. Don't look for things in your partner that can be found only in God.
- *Be content.* Hollywood perpetuates the idea of the 'soulmate'. This is the idea that there is only one person out there who is perfect for you. If you find him or her, you will have a trouble-free relationship. But it's a myth. We are to choose our love and then love our choice. Be satisfied with 'the wife of your youth' (Proverbs 5:18).
- *Be realistic.* Do not sacrifice a good marriage because you want a perfect one. It is wise to work hard to make our marriage the best it can be, but don't spoil it by perfectionism.
- *Don't compare.* Every marriage is unique. When we compare ourselves with others, it is sure to lead to disappointment. We see the good things, but are unaware of the battles others had to fight to get to where they are. Work at what works for you.
- *Invest the pain.* The trials of marriage can be profound, but if we invest them wisely, they can lead to fruit that will last. Like all disappointment, use trials as stepping stones to greater self-knowledge and a firmer trust in the faithfulness of God.
- *Look beyond the current circumstances.* Remember, your circumstances don't define you. God does. Don't allow temporary disappointment to cut you off from the joy that God gives.

- *Don't be selfish.* See your marriage as an opportunity for service. Use your home as an outpost of the kingdom of God. In marriage we learn that the way to find life is to give it away, and the way to happiness is the way of sacrifice.
- *Cultivate friendship.* Maintain a wide variety of appropriate friendships. Let people in.
- *Stay faithful.* Flee from the temptation to find your emotional needs met by someone other than your partner. Disappointment can make us vulnerable, and the lure of an emotionally sensitive friend can be very seductive. Be on your guard and nip wrong activity in the bud.

A marriage based on a common commitment to Jesus offers great joy. It may feel like 'dancing in the minefields' and 'sailing in the storms',[6] if I can mix my metaphors, but God promises to be faithful to those who are faithful to him.

Will it hurt? You bet. Is it worth it? Of course it is!

Questions

1. Why does God give us friends?
2. What are the challenges and advantages of singleness?
3. What do we seek for in another person that can be found only in God?
4. If you are married, work together through the bullet points in the last section. Do they make sense? How do they apply to you right now?
5. If you are not married, do the same exercise, but adapt it and apply it to your friendships.

6. Parents in pain: when our children break our hearts

As she approached me, she was obviously nervous and somewhat distressed.

It was a large Christian conference, and I had just finished delivering a paper on the biblical view of homosexuality. I had tried to be faithful to the clear biblical teaching that sexual intimacy is to be confined to marriage, defined by God as involving one man and one woman in a lifelong commitment of love and faithfulness. At the same time, I had affirmed the importance of compassion and the need to treat our neighbour with respect and dignity.

I thought that I had got the balance between grace and truth just about right. But then, after a preamble, she asked her question:

Thank you for your paper. I agree with everything you said.
I have one son and I love him to bits. He is in his second year at university and he came home at Christmas and told me that he is gay. Here is my question: as a Christian, am I still allowed to love him?

'Of course you should love him,' I assured her.

But afterwards I felt shaken. Had I got things so wrong that I had provoked such a thought? I looked at my notes and I wasn't sure. Maybe her sense of pain had clouded the way she heard what I was saying. Whatever the reality, I decided that in future I would be careful to emphasize grace, without abandoning biblical integrity.

But this incident is just one illustration of a much wider issue.

How do we cope with the disappointment that comes when, for whatever reason, our children break our hearts? It is a much more common problem than we imagine. Churches are full of disappointed parents.

We are not supposed to live our lives through our kids. Some of our expectations are unrealistic and even cruel. There is something unhealthy about seeking to live off the prestige that their successes bring. We need to give them roots and wings: roots for stability and wings for independence and freedom.

However, the disappointment caused by our children often represents some of the most profound suffering that we will ever experience. Sometimes it comes as a huge shock to the system when delightful kids become rebellious teenagers. I once overheard someone saying, 'When my son was a baby he was so lovely – I could have eaten him. When he became a teenager, I wish I had done!'

But it is no joke. Among the most painful and disappointing experiences of life are those shared by parents in pain.

Children: a blessing from God

But let's begin with the obvious – children are a blessing!

They are a gift from God (Psalm 127:3–5), included among the good gifts that come down from the hand of a generous heavenly Father. We are to honour them and welcome them, as Jesus did (Mark 9:37).

Of course, there are frustrating challenges in parenting: sleepless nights, temper tantrums and sibling rivalry, to name just three. But there are also extraordinary moments of joy and pride. Children are not a mistake or an accident. God determines the day of their birth (Psalm 139:16) and knew them before they were born (Jeremiah 1:5).

Jesus used children as an example of discipleship:

> He called a little child to him, and placed the child among them. And he said: 'Truly I tell you, unless you change and become like little children, you will never enter the kingdom of heaven. Therefore, whoever takes the lowly position of this child is the greatest in the kingdom of heaven. And whoever welcomes one such child in my name welcomes me.'
> (Matthew 18:2–5)

We need to treat them with love and respect, and indeed, Jesus reserves his severest warnings for those who abuse or misuse children:

> If anyone causes one of these little ones – those who believe in me – to stumble, it would be better for them to have a large millstone hung round their neck and to be drowned in the depths of the sea.
> (Matthew 18:6)

God's design and intention for most married couples is the blessing of children. But what if that blessing never happens?

The pain of infertility

Earlier I shared something of the devastating experience of my wife's miscarriage. The pain was intense and felt just as profound as any other form of grief. But within a relatively short period of time we had the comfort of the birth of our first son, with others to follow.

But what about when there are no children to bring consolation and gladness? What if you can never conceive? What if conception is possible but it never reaches full term? Among some of the greatest disappointments in life are those associated with child-lessness. How do you cope when one treatment after another fails? How much longer do you keep going? And there are always those 'helpful' Christians who will remind you of Sarah or Elizabeth in the Bible – they had to wait for years, but in the end God gave them children. Just have faith!

The Bible takes the pain of infertility seriously:

The leech has two daughters.
'Give! Give!' they cry.
'There are three things that are never satisfied,
    four that never say, "Enough!":
the grave, the barren womb,
    land, which is never satisfied with water,
    and fire, which never says, "Enough!"'
(Proverbs 30:15–16)

Infertility can cause an ocean of grief, and it is not 'unspiritual' to feel a consequent profound sense of loss. I have seen it tear people apart and put marriages under intense pressure. I have known women who could not come to the Mothers' Day services at church, and others who would avoid going anywhere near the crèche. Increasing anxiety to conceive can also destroy the normal enjoyment of sexual intercourse between husband and wife.

Part of the problem is that our society gives us the impression that it is our right to have children. Advances in reproductive technologies convince us that pregnancy is within the grasp of any woman. Motherhood is a rite of passage – how can I be a real woman if I cannot even have a baby? How can I be a real man if I cannot give my wife the child she so desperately longs for? Having a child is often seen as the entrance fee to certain social groups at church or in society. Childlessness, by contrast, gives a sense of exclusion.

The Bible and infertility

The Bible contains several examples of infertile couples who finally conceive. Think of Abraham and Sarah, or Elizabeth and Zechariah. In most cases you will notice that the child to be born is part of God's plan to bring about redemption for the world. Isaac, Samson, Samuel and John the Baptist all had a vital role in God's purposes. The birth of these children is an indication of God's power to do the impossible, and to assure us that his purposes cannot fail. In the case of John the Baptist, it is to prepare us for the even greater miracle of the virgin birth.

What does all this mean? We cannot take these stories to teach believers that every couple has a divinely given right to have children. The Bible is not a textbook about infertility.

In the Old Testament the first command God gave to humans was to be fruitful and multiply, and to exercise dominion over the creation. In the New Testament the command to the church is to make disciples of all nations. While children are still a wonderful blessing from God, having children is not the only way God has ordained and blessed for the leaving of a heritage.

Infertility is not a punishment from God. This needs to be said loudly and clearly. At the time of writing, my wife has suffered with severe neurological illness for twenty-five years. It has only recently been diagnosed as multiple sclerosis. We have been told more than once that it is because of lack of faith or some secret sin that God is punishing her for. We are pretty much immune to this kind of theological misinformation now. But it has taken time. When a couple cannot conceive, they are often similarly vulnerable to unhelpful misdirection. The fact that you do not have a child is certainly not an indication that there is something spiritually amiss.

As with all the forms of disappointment we have already explored in this book, the answer to the problem is to find our ultimate satisfaction in God himself. It is easy for children to take God's place and become the ultimate idol in our lives.

The Bible is full of glorious promises, such as the following:

> The LORD is close to the broken-hearted
>   and saves those who are crushed in spirit.
> (Psalm 34:18)

In the gospel, through Jesus, God gives us himself. In God we find the comfort we need. The church, as we know by now, should be a place where we come to know the joy of family. Jesus invites us into the spiritual fellowship of the church, which supersedes even earthly family ties:

> He replied to him, 'Who is my mother, and who are my brothers?' Pointing to his disciples, he said, 'Here are my mother and my brothers. For whoever does the will of my Father in heaven is my brother and sister and mother.'
> (Matthew 12:48–50)

And just as single people escape the challenges of married life, so childless couples escape the pain that children can bring. This is so, even though, in the midst of either of these situations, people might easily say, 'I don't care – give me that pain if it means that I will marry / have a child!'

The gravity of parental love

So what are the challenges that parents face?

There is a kind of gravity about love that you do not properly appreciate until you become a parent.

What I mean is that love flows downwards from one generation to the next. The flow goes both ways, but the torrent is uneven. We love our parents and long for their affirmation. As we grow up, we learn what it is to move out of their shadow and we begin to find our independence and freedom. Of course, we still love them, but the focus of our deeper affections moves elsewhere. That is natural and right. As they get older, we may be called upon to show the patience and love that we ourselves experienced as children.

But for parents, the moment this tiny squalling cosmos is placed in our arms, we know that life has changed for ever. Parenting is a lifelong commitment. As we love our own children, we come to see that that is how our parents loved us, even though we did not realize it at the time.

There is no love quite like parental love – and there is no pain quite like parental pain. Our children can disappoint and neglect us and break our hearts, and we will still go on loving them. The Bible contains numerous examples of the pain that children bring to the hearts of parents. Remember the death of Abel at the hands of his brother (Genesis 4:1–16), or the sibling rivalry between the sons of Isaac and Rebekah (Genesis 26:34 – 27:46). Think of the distress Eli's sons brought to his heart (1 Samuel 2:12–25), or the pain that Absalom caused David (2 Samuel 18:19 – 19:8).

As we reflect on this, perhaps we can enter the heart of God. His love to us is always greater than our love for him. Indeed, our waywardness often wounds him deeply.

Hosea, prophesying to a nation that has rejected God, picks up this image in graphic terms. God had loved Israel as a father loves a child, but his son has rebelled against him:

> When Israel was a child, I loved him,
>   and out of Egypt I called my son.
> But the more they were called,
>   the more they went away from me.

> They sacrificed to the Baals
>   and they burned incense to images.
> It was I who taught Ephraim to walk,
>   taking them by the arms;
> but they did not realize
>   it was I who healed them.
> I led them with cords of human kindness,
>   with ties of love.
> To them I was like one who lifts
>   a little child to the cheek,
>   and I bent down to feed them.
> (Hosea 11:1–4)

He is tempted to reject his son completely and turn his back on him. But then, in one of the most moving passages in Scripture, God bares his heart before his people:

> How can I give you up, Ephraim?
>   How can I hand you over, Israel?
> How can I treat you like Admah?
>   How can I make you like Zeboyim?
> My heart is changed within me;
>   all my compassion is aroused.
> I will not carry out my fierce anger,
>   nor will I devastate Ephraim again.
> For I am God, and not a man –
>   the Holy One among you.
>   I will not come against their cities.
> (Hosea 11:8–9)

Like a parent in pain, God expresses the anguish of a broken heart. And yet he will not turn away from the child who has rejected him so consistently and blatantly.

Parents as ambassadors

Bringing up kids in today's world demands wisdom, grace, perseverance and, of course, a good sense of humour. At every stage there will be a new challenge. We need to guard our homes and protect our children from the pressures, disappointments and conflicts of life. We need to live out our faith before them and help them to understand what it means to us. At the same time we need to prepare them for the future and for the time when they will leave us and launch out on their own.

Perhaps the most important thing we can do for our children is create a community of grace in the home, where they can experience the kindness and goodness of God. We have come to know that the Lord is slow to anger and compassionate towards us. We have felt the tenderness of his heart. Our children need to taste the same sort of kindness that we crave from God. We are 'ambassadors of God's grace' in the lives of our children.

Pastor and author Paul Tripp observes,

> Parents, allow yourself to reflect on how much you need God's
> mercy now, reflect on how much you needed the mercy of
> your parents as you grew up, and let sympathy grow in your
> heart. Mercy means that every action, reaction, and response
> toward your children is tempered and shaped by tenderness,
> understanding, compassion, and love. Parenting is a life-long
> mission of humbly, joyfully, and willingly giving mercy.[1]

Of course, we are to exercise kind and gracious discipline so that children understand the connection between sin and pain. We are responsible for the atmosphere in our homes (Ephesians 6:4). At the same time, we must nurture children in a culture of grace. If you make mistakes, apologize and ask for forgiveness. When they say sorry, don't keep a record of wrong. Don't be overprotective and don't be over-tolerant. Don't provoke your children to anger – know them well enough to understand what makes them angry. If you are over-critical, they will lose heart (Colossians 3:21).

And remember how quickly time goes – don't wish it away. Enjoy the times that you have with them. You can be physically present and yet functionally absent. Really be there for them, and delight in them.

Prodigal children

We mostly experience prodigal children when they reject our faith and walk away from God.

But within this there is a wide spectrum of experience. On the one hand, there are those children who are respectable and respectful and who have chosen to live a life in which God does not figure. They might walk the fence spiritually, wanting to please their parents, play by the rules and still come to church, but they have no inner life from God. On the other hand, there is the rebellious son or daughter who throws off all constraints and lives in extreme defiance and rebellion. This may involve disrespect, deceit and even self-destruction.

The pain will be more immediate and obvious in the second case. But the underlying problem is the same. As a Christian parent, I long for my kids to know Jesus and live for him. I have an eye to eternity. The Bible is clear about the eternal realities of heaven and hell. As parents, we are of course delighted when our kids find a good partner or succeed in their chosen career or present us with grandchildren. But our deepest longing is that they will share heaven with us, and our deepest disappointment is when they discount God and reject the gospel we hold so dear.

And I guess that this is where we often feel the most profound guilt about our parenting. We know that our kids are born with sinful hearts and they need to experience God's grace personally. Our faith is not passed on in the genes. But when our children do not come to faith, we often blame ourselves. I was too strict;

I wasn't strict enough. I talked about God too much; I didn't share my faith enough. I was too anxious; I was too laid-back. It is easy for disappointment to lead to grief, and for grief to turn into guilt. We carry it around like a millstone.

It is true that, as parents, we have a right and responsibility to teach our children the faith (2 Timothy 1:5; Deuteronomy 6:6–9). We should pray for them, direct their steps, live a Christlike life before them and not provoke them to anger (Proverbs 23:13–14; 29:17; Ephesians 6:4; Colossians 3:21). However, no careful observation of biblical principles can ensure the salvation of our children. They are responsible for their own decisions. Their hearts are always outside our control. A wise father sometimes has a foolish daughter, and a godly mother may have an ungodly son. Only God can change hearts and bring about the salvation of our children. Only he can open their hearts (Acts 16:14–15). We cannot control their hearts – but God can!

Practical suggestions for parents in pain

So how do we respond as parents of prodigals? Or how do we help parents suffering with the disappointment of a wayward child? Here are some practical suggestions:

- *Acknowledge that something is wrong.* Don't be afraid or embarrassed to admit that you have a problem. Don't ignore the signs or refuse to accept that it is true. If your children reject Christ, don't pretend that this is fine. And if they are not Christians, don't expect them to be Christlike in their behaviour.
- *Love them lavishly.* Tell them that you love them. Use affirming words, meaningful hugs and quality time. Be gentle in your disappointment. Don't accept their sin, but balance truth with grace. Remind them that they are always your kids and, however hard it gets, never walk

away. Plead with them rather than rebuking them. God's relentless love is our model (Isaiah 54:10).

- *Pray for them passionately.* Entrust them to God – he loves them more than you do. Be honest with God and tell him how you feel. Since it is the divine prerogative to save, pray for their conversion. God can do more than you imagine (Ephesians 3:20–21). Why not start a prayer group at church for parents in pain?

- *Point them to Christ.* Aim for their conversion, not simply that they become 'good kids'. Don't concentrate on externals – the real problem is not tattoos or hair length or loud music, but that they don't see Jesus clearly. Show them Jesus so that they are captivated by his love and satisfied with him alone. Demonstrate the love of Jesus to them.

- *Grow through your pain.* One of the reasons why God gives us teenagers is to sanctify us. Like all disappointments, this one is designed to deal with the problems of our heart. Our kids can become idols – we must love God more than we love them (Matthew 10:37). Be real with God, other people and your children.

- *Continue to connect with them.* Keep in touch. Communicate with them constantly. Avoid cold body language and harsh words. Send emails, texts, Facebook messages. Take them out for a meal – not all communication needs to be electronic! Be interested in what interests them. Respect their friends, who, in turn, may be someone else's prodigals. Nothing is solved by showing them how much you disapprove. Jesus was the friend of sinners (Luke 7:36–50).

- *Don't be too proud to ask for help.* Seek help from others – emotional support, spiritual wisdom and professional help. Look to your own parents and mature Christians for support. Pray that your kids will have contact with other Christians.

- *Offer them a haven.* The home is an outpost for the kingdom of God. Assure them that they do not need to earn your love, and don't expect perfection when they return. The prodigal son still smelled of the pigsty, but the father did not mention the smell. He put clean robes on top of rags, a ring on a dirty finger and clean sandals on smelly feet. Remember that your children are more ashamed than you are. If they go back to church, pray that they will meet the father before they encounter the older brother.

- *Guard your marriage and your family.* Don't allow prodigal children to drive a wedge between you and your spouse. Rather, build a united front. Guard your family – don't sacrifice your other children either. Set boundaries and do not accept destructive behaviour or abandon your core values. Allow yourself to enjoy life – rest, work and play. Don't go into 'suspended animation' until things are resolved.

- *Be patient.* Be patient in your waiting, and don't get impatient with God. We may watch our children reach adulthood and have children of their own. It's all too easy to despair and stop praying. Don't give up. Walk by faith and don't become weary in doing good (2 Corinthians 5:7; Galatians 6:9). God is the only perfect parent – you can trust him. You can still be fattening the calf, even if the prodigal has not returned home yet. God may surprise you!

Loving God most

Jesus taught his disciples that their love for him must supersede all earthly ties:

> Anyone who loves their father or mother more than me is not worthy of me; anyone who loves their son or daughter more

than me is not worthy of me. Whoever does not take up their cross and follow me is not worthy of me. Whoever finds their life will lose it, and whoever loses their life for my sake will find it. (Matthew 10:37–39)

This is biblical Christianity.

We have a history with our children. They are an ever-present reality, touching our lives in powerful ways. God, on the other hand, is invisible, and we do not always feel the immediacy and intensity of emotion that loving our children brings us.

However, we must make the choice every day to find our satisfaction in God and not in others. The distresses of infertility or the agony of having a wayward child awaken us to the stark reality that true fulfilment is found in God alone.

And it is only as we love God that we can love our children as we should.

Questions

1. Why do we invest so much emotional capital in our children?
2. How should the church support those who struggle with infertility?
3. There is a gravity about love. Do you agree? What are the implications for the way we think about our relationship with God and with our parents?
4. How do we go about creating a 'community of grace' in our home? How does this apply if we are single, or married and childless?
5. You almost certainly know someone with a prodigal child, if you yourself do not have one. Work through the bullet points in the section on 'Practical suggestions for parents in pain'. How can you best support those who struggle with this problem?

7. Loving what Jesus loves: when church distresses us and leaders shock us

We have a regular slot for children in our morning service. I like to give the impression that I am now way too old to talk to the kids, but secretly I cherish the opportunity. And I can usually find something that fits in with the theme of the service, to be enjoyed by the adults as much as the children.

But on occasions I'm not quite sure about a talk, so I ask my wife's advice. Will this be on their wavelength? Is it suitable? Will it work?

A couple of years ago I came up with what I thought was a stonking kids' talk. I wanted to illustrate the importance of belonging to the local church and had decided to make it as visual as possible. I would call the children to the front and then produce a carving knife. I would then ask if they would like me to cut off the little finger on my left hand. Of course, they would say 'no'. I would then tell them that Christians are joined to the body of Christ. If we are severed from church fellowship for any reason, then we can shrivel up and die. If you amputate a finger, it is painful for the body, but it is absolutely fatal for the finger!

What a brilliant illustration! I was so proud of it, but thought that I had better check it out with Edrie first. I presented it to her as dramatically as I could, and waited for the applause.

After a moment of stunned silence, her derision was unconcealed: 'Are you insane? Use your imagination! What do you think will happen? Half the kids will be traumatized, and their parents will be furious with you. The other half will be deeply disappointed that you have not delivered on your promises and removed the finger. What were you thinking?'

I tried a few feeble arguments, but quickly came to see that she was probably right. A higher wisdom prevailed, so the talk was never given.

But I still grieve over it.

It really is a fine illustration of a biblical truth, even if entirely inappropriate for the under-tens! The Bible makes it clear that being joined to Christ means being joined to the local church. If I cut myself off from the fellowship of God's people, the church will suffer from my absence. But it will be absolutely fatal for my spiritual life. What use is an amputated finger? You could keep it in the deep freezer and occasionally produce it for children's talks, but even I can see that that is too gruesome. Cut off from the life-sustaining vitality of the local church, we too will shrivel up spiritually.

In short, we need the church.

But herein lies a problem. Often people have been so badly damaged by the local church that, rather than being a source of comfort, encouragement and joy, it has become a place of pain, fear and heartbreak. We can even become damaged and hindered from following Christ.

So what do you do when you are disappointed with the church?

When church becomes toxic

Church is supposed to be a place where we learn to grow as Christians.

I had the great blessing of growing up in a healthy Christian fellowship. It wasn't perfect, but it was warm, loving and nurturing. The teaching was biblical, balanced and life-giving. I respected and trusted the leaders and was happy to follow their lead. Looking back, I can remember some discussions where conflicting opinions were expressed, even forcefully on occasions, but they never breached the bonds of loving fellowship. We could disagree without being disagreeable!

I think that it was when I moved to my second church that it really dawned on me that not all churches are like that. The church I worked for was like the church I had grown up in, but I had not been there long before we began to encounter what I can only describe as 'Christian casualties'. It was easy to identify them. They would turn up on a Sunday and leave as quickly as possible. They were very reluctant to engage, and when I offered to visit, they were obviously suspicious of my agenda. Sometimes they came for a while and would then disappear entirely. But eventually, after I had assured them that the church was a safe place, some managed to open up and share their stories.

What I discovered was that there was a massive group of people so badly damaged by the church that they found it hard to imagine one that could be anything other than toxic. These guys had come from a whole range of backgrounds. Some had been part of groups that were obviously cultic, but others were from what we might identify as mainstream Christian groups. Their stories were varied, and the damage they had experienced was of different levels of intensity. Sometimes I concluded that the fault lay as much with them as with the church. But there were many examples of real disciples of Jesus who had been exploited and injured in the very place where they should have been cherished and nourished. Some managed to recover and become healthy members of our church. But others never made it – they either drifted from one church to another, or they gave up on church entirely.

As I got to know their stories, certain common features emerged.

Sometimes they had been marred by the acrimony generated by a divided church. They had come looking for love and had found party spirit, poisonous discord and a steady stream of harmful words. Sadly, when Christians fall out, they often behave worse than non-Christians. I have been in churches where you can feel the chill of division, even at Communion. In such a situation it is easy to despair. It was the arch-atheist Friedrich Nietzsche who is reputed to have said, 'You Christians will have to look a lot more like Christ if I am to believe in him.'

Sometimes there is a lack of balance in the church's teaching. Law is preached, and there is little place for grace. Failure is final, and there is no way back for those who have not reached some external form of man-made legalism. Some churches are deeply committed to truth, but there is no place for love. Sometimes secondary issues are proclaimed as primary issues, and woe betide you if you question the preacher's infallibility.

Some churches work hard at being loving communities and yet seem too willing to sacrifice objective truth on the altar of utility. Others are sounder than the apostles, but rigid and cold and as loveless as the grave. The variation on this theme is almost endless.

But if there is one issue that presents itself more commonly than any other, it is in the whole area of leadership.

When leadership is lethal

The most common thread in people's stories was on the damage that unbalanced and unhealthy leaders could do.

Of course, God blesses us by sending us good and godly leaders. Leadership is vital to the health of the church and the attainment of its mission. When Israel cried out to God from the terrible furnace of suffering in Egypt, God remembered his covenant promises to them and sent them Moses (Exodus 3:7–10). Later they entered the land of promise under the firm and effective leadership of Joshua. The nation fragmented when it had no king (Judges 17:6; 18:1; 19:1; 21:25). After the establishment of the monarchy, the fate of the nation was inexorably linked with the character of the kings who ruled in God's name. The great tragedy of their history was that most of their kings proved to be unfaithful shepherds (Ezekiel 34:1–6).

In the New Testament Jesus invested much of his time training the apostles to lead the church. After Pentecost the apostles give clear and courageous leadership to the young church (Acts 5:27–32). Christian missionaries make sure that every new church has a strong leadership team in place (Acts 14:23; Titus 1:5). Paul invests a lot of time training and preparing a new generation of leaders and is concerned that they should share his vision (2 Timothy 2:2).

We have a responsibility to respect our leaders and to follow their direction (Hebrews 13:7, 17–18). A number have been badly treated and wounded by their churches. If we find ourselves causing grief to those whom God has gifted to lead his church, we will need to repent and put things right.

But in many cases the fault lies with the leader rather than the led. It is easy for leaders to overstep the biblical guidelines and demand an allegiance and a devotion that belongs to God alone. There are obvious cases where the leader exploits a position to abuse the members of a congregation emotionally, financially or sexually. As 'the Lord's anointed', such leaders are beyond contradiction, and any attack on their authority is tantamount to an attack on God himself. Such cases are usually easy to diagnose and identify.

However, it is sometimes less obvious. So how do you know when a leader has stepped over the line? How do I know if my leadership is becoming lethal?

Here are some questions for a leader to ask:

- Do I expect people to follow my leadership without question just because I say so? Do I get angry when they don't?
- Do I resent my fellow leaders when they disagree with me? Do I demand a position of pre-eminence among those with whom I serve?
- Do I admit my faults to the congregation? Do I apologize when I get things wrong? Do I use my congregation to boost my ego, or is my real passion the glory of God?
- How do I cope with criticism?
- Do I take myself too seriously? Can I laugh at myself?
- Do I look for people to follow me, or do I want them to follow Jesus? Do I look for an allegiance that should belong to God alone?
- Do I see myself as the servant of Christ and of his people? Do I love them enough to lay down my life for them?

What about the person in the pew? How do I know when my leader is overstepping the mark?

Christians are often loyal people, and we want to follow the biblical injunction to submit to our leaders:

> Have confidence in your leaders and submit to their authority, because they keep watch over you as those who must give an account. Do this so that their work will be a joy, not a burden, for that would be of no benefit to you.
> (Hebrews 13:17)

Quite honestly, who wants to become a burden? Leaders do have a God-given authority and they are answerable to God for the faithful discharge of their ministries. The church is not a democracy – Christ is Lord of his church and he exercises authority through leaders who submit to the dictates of his word.

However, there are limits. The best advice I can give you is to respect and honour your leaders, but never give your conscience to any person other than God. The authority that God has established in the church, the home and the world all sits under the overall lordship of Jesus Christ. So, for example, Christians are to respect and obey the state – rulers are ordained by God (Romans 13:1–7). But what if the state demands what belongs to God?

When Peter and John are forbidden to proclaim Christ, their response is very clear: 'Which is right in God's eyes: to listen to you, or to him? You be the judges! As for us, we cannot help speaking about what we have seen and heard' (Acts 4:18–19).

The same applies in the home and in the church. Indeed, in whatever network of relationships we find ourselves, our ultimate allegiance must be to God. I cannot submit my mind and conscience to anyone other than Christ.

Now I know that some of us are awkward characters, who will take this as an excuse for questioning everything that our leaders want to do. This is not a justification for stubborn, stroppy and uncooperative behaviour! But good leaders who are comfortable in their skin and confident about their position in Christ will be open to constructive criticism and recognize that they do not have a monopoly of wisdom.

The stain that remains

And what happens when a trusted and loved Christian leader falls into the chasm of moral failure? We naturally feel betrayed and deceived and even shattered.

'He was the one who buried my wife.'

'She led me to the Lord.'

'I trusted him with my deepest secrets.'

'Was he always a deceiver?'

'Was there ever a time when she was not a hypocrite?'

'How could I have been so naive – so stupid as to trust him?'

'How could he be so brash and brazen about it?'

'If the heart of the servant is wrong, how can we ever trust their message? And is Christianity, after all, just a con trick?'

It is not wrong to have heroes in the faith – Christians who inspire us by their example and encourage us by their words. Paul could say to the Corinthian church, 'Follow my example, as I follow the example of Christ' (1 Corinthians 11:1).

We invest trust and commitment in our leaders, but what happens when we discover that they have feet of clay? A relatively minor lapse can jolt us and shake our faith. But what happens when the failure is so serious that it leads to an exit from ministry? Churches become polarized, and their testimony is besmirched. The media delights in chronicling the spectacular downfall of leaders, of course. But perhaps the greatest pain of all is felt by individual believers in the congregation.

This is not the place to explore the dynamics of leadership failure. Some leaders were never converted in the first place, while others are genuine believers who have fallen into sin and are horrified by the consequences of their actions. Some have been keeping secrets and wearing a mask for a long time, while others are using their failure as a means of escape from a ministry that has ended up exhausting and demoralizing them.

How do we deal with the devastating disappointment that this brings?

Here are some suggestions:

- *Remember that your leaders are sinners saved by the grace of God.* Like every Christian, they are imperfect and prone to sin. Don't become a Pharisee: remember that any of us, the leaders or the led, is capable of serious moral failure.
- *Focus on Jesus* – he is the only true and perfect leader. The closer you get to people, the more you will see their faults. Respect them, but do not give them unqualified regard, something that should be reserved for Jesus alone. He will never disappoint you – you really can trust him.

- *Make sure that you distinguish the message from the messenger.* God can draw a straight line with a crooked stick. Jesus entrusted the gospel to imperfect people. The original apostles were a bunch of deserters, deniers and doubters. The message itself is one of amazing grace. God graciously uses those who desperately need his grace in order to propagate it.
- *However, don't opt for 'cheap grace'.* There is a debate about the possibility of restoration after moral failure. This is not the place to enter that debate, but whichever side we come down on, we must never minimize sin. Those who speak God's word will be judged more seriously (James 3:1–2). God is concerned both with the fidelity of the message and the integrity of the messenger. Sin always has consequences.
- *Don't torture yourself by trying to understand how a moral lapse happened.* You cannot see into another person's soul.
- *Put away bitterness and cynicism.* These emotions will eat away at you like acid. As Christians, we are to give them no place. Ask God to help you to learn to forgive, even as you too have been forgiven.
- *Don't doubt your previous experience.* It is often the memory of past blessings that caused the most acute pain in the present. You do not have to doubt the authenticity of that moment. The failure of the messenger does not nullify the truthfulness of the message. In his grace, God is at work even in the mess and mire of human life.
- *Turn your disappointment into passionate prayer.* Pray for those who have fallen – that God would reach them in their rebellion and restore their relationship with him. Pray for their marriage and their family. Pray for your church. Pray that God would turn even this dire situation into good.

God's view of the church

If I have been disappointed with the church, what should I do?

A good starting place is to develop a balanced understanding of the nature of the church in its present existence. The New Testament says many things about the church, but I'll focus on two.

First, it stresses the mystery and majesty, the wonder and glory of the church. In this present age the church is central to the purpose of God and at the heart of all that he wants to do in this world. In just one New Testament book, Paul's letter to the Ephesians, there are at least ten passages that deal with the nature of the church:

- Christ has been exalted to the ultimate place of authority in the universe and he now rules over all things for the sake of the church, which is his body, the fullness of him who fills everything in every way (1:18–23).
- The church is the place where human divisions are destroyed and people are reconciled through the cross (2:14–18).
- The church is the spiritual temple where God now dwells by his Spirit (2:19–22).
- In the church, God's wisdom – the plan by which he will bring about the unity of all things under the headship of Christ – is displayed to the cosmos (3:10–13).
- The church is the place where his glory is displayed (3:20–21).
- The church has been created by God and is united by his Spirit (4:1–6).
- The church is blessed with the gifts that God has bestowed on it and it is a place of amazing variety and healthy diversity (4:7–16).
- The church is a place where wholesome talk and gracious relationships are to build us up in our faith (4:29 – 5:2).

- The church is the bride of Christ. He loved her and gave his life for her. One day he will perfect her (5:25–33).
- The church is a mighty army called to stand firm against the dark forces of this world (6:10–20).

Christ loved the church and gave himself up for her. The proof of our love for him is our love for his people (1 John 2:9–11; 3:11–20; 4:7–12, 19). The New Testament has no conception of a Christian who exists outside the warm embrace of the local church (Hebrews 10:24–25). Indeed, the mission of Christ is the mission of the church – she illustrates the amazing love of God that breaks down human barriers. She demonstrates before a watching world the power and grace of God (John 13:34–35).

But in reality . . .

And then you have the local church with all its faults and foibles.

Have you ever visited a church that resembled the kind of church that Paul describes above? Is it just a fantasy? If only we could get back to the church of the first century, then we would become what the church ought to be. And, of course, renewal and restoration movements down through the ages have always tried to do just that.

We really do want to see the church refreshed and restored. The Reformers were right about the need to return to the glorious simplicity of the apostolic gospel. But was the church ever perfect?

The second thing that the New Testament is clear about in its teaching on this subject is that no perfect church has ever existed. Every church is in constant need of repentance and change.

Paul, who wrote Ephesians, also wrote 1 Corinthians. This letter reveals that just about everything that could go wrong in the church has gone wrong in Corinth:

- There was serious disunity and division, probably based on a personality cult (1:10–11).

- The church was guilty of serious sexual sin (5:1–5, 9–10). Even pagans were shocked!
- People had fallen out with each other and were taking one another to court, rather than settling matters in a gracious and loving way (6:1–8).
- Believers were puffed up with pride about their knowledge (8:1–2).
- The Lord's Table (Communion) had become a place of chaotic division (11:17–34).
- There was jealousy and pride about spiritual gifts (12:16–22).
- There were even some who were unsure about the resurrection of Christ (15:12–18).

And yet Paul does not write them off. He recognizes that they are young believers having to shed a lot of baggage as they learn to be faithful disciples of Christ. They may have had zeal without wisdom – but at least they were exuberant in their faith, and the problems of the church were the problems of life rather than the problems of death. They appear to have been making a real impact on the world, and people from all sorts of backgrounds were being transformed by the grace of God (6:9–11). Above everything else, they were teachable. They were open to Paul's direction and, we can see from 2 Corinthians, many of the issues he addressed would be dealt with.

And Corinth was not alone.

Every New Testament church had its blind spots and glaring faults. At the very end of the first century, Jesus assesses the seven churches of Asia Minor. Two get an almost faultless report, but there are serious issues in the other five. One has lost its first love; another has the appearance of life, but is nearly dead. One is so compromised that it makes Jesus sick (Revelation 2 – 3). Once again there are severe warnings, but Jesus does not write them off.

And this pattern has repeated itself during the millennia of the church's existence. The perfect church does not exist. This is because the church is made up of people like you and me – imperfect individuals struggling to serve Jesus and often failing. Multiply my faults by your faults, and add them together with the faults of a multitude of diverse people and then corral them together in the narrow confines of the local church! No wonder there are problems.

Martin Luther got it right:

> May a merciful God preserve me from a Christian Church in which everyone is a saint! I want to be and remain in the church and little flock of the fainthearted, the feeble and the ailing, who feel and recognize the wretchedness of their sins, who sigh and cry to God incessantly for comfort and help, who believe in the forgiveness of sins.[1]

Back to church – love what God loves

So how do I cope when I am disappointed with the church? Here are my suggestions:

- *You may need to get out!* Some churches are in fact toxic. Don't stay out of a sense of fear or misplaced loyalty. Remember the test: are they asking you to surrender your conscience? If so, then do not stay.
- *Don't drift.* You need to find a church. Don't set the bar so high that no church could ever qualify. Don't become an amputated digit in the deep freezer.
- *Examine your own heart.* Some people struggle with any form of submission to authority. Is that you? If you discover that you are part of the awkward squad, then repent and ask God to give you a humble heart. Learn to trust the leaders. If you have been manipulated in the

past, this might prove difficult. Ask God to give you a
thick skin and a tender heart.

- *Learn to forgive.* It is one of the hardest things God tells
  us to do. It is also one of the most necessary. There is no
  future in bitterness.
- *Hang in there.* All churches will have ups and downs. The
  closer you get, the more obvious the blemishes become.
  But you need to persevere and become part of the solution
  rather than part of the problem.
- *Love the church for all its faults and foibles.* Remember that
  Jesus loved it enough to die for it. So don't bad-mouth his
  bride!
- *Think about what the church will one day become.* If you lead
  a church, aim to build a community of grace where love
  and truth are equally important. If you are looking for
  a church, try to find somewhere where you can grow
  through the teaching of God's word, build a few deep and
  healthy relationships and get involved in a specific area of
  ministry.

Here's a story that I related in a previous book which illustrates
the above very well.

I once visited an elderly Christian couple in a care home. I
chatted with the husband while his wife slept. When she woke
up, she reached for her Zimmer frame. As she slowly crossed the
room towards us, with one stocking around her ankle and
the marks of sleep still resting in the corners of her eyes, he
turned to me, his face suffused with pride.

'That's my girl,' he said in a broad Wiltshire accent. 'Isn't she
beautiful?'

It is all a matter of perspective. He saw what I, even in my
most chivalrous mood, couldn't see. He loved her and he saw
beauty. Christ loves the church and is preparing an eternity of
bliss for her. We need to see the big picture. We need to see the
church through his eyes.[2]

One day his purpose for his church will reach perfection, and she will be 'without stain or wrinkle or any other blemish, but holy and blameless' (Ephesians 5:25–27).

That's the big picture, and in the midst of the battle we need to see this.

Questions

1. Why do we need to be fully engaged with a local church? What will happen to us if we do not engage?
2. How do I guard my conscience? How do I know when someone is demanding that which belongs to God alone?
3. How do we learn to forgive those who have damaged us?
4. If you are a leader, work though the bullet points under the section, 'When leadership is lethal'. Does anything here alarm you?
5. Jesus loves the church, but his love is not blind. How should this affect the way we view church?

8. The enemy within: when we are disillusioned with ourselves

What do we do when our greatest disappointment is not with other people but with ourselves? When the greatest enemy is the enemy within?

I think of Graham (not his real name, and I have his permission to tell his story).

Graham came to my weekly surgery when I was a pastor in the Midlands. I could tell just by looking at him that he was in a real state. He had been a Christian for two years. Before his conversion he had been a happy addict of pornography. Occasionally it troubled him – but not much. The first thing that happened after his conversion was that he realized that it was foul and he stopped immediately. Other guys I have counselled have struggled with porn for years, but Graham seemed to find deliverance immediately. And for eighteen months he was completely and almost effortlessly porn-free. Then trouble at work and a couple of discouragements at church seemed to make him vulnerable to temptation, and he found himself thinking about the release that porn used to bring. It seems to offer instant stress-free gratification without the complications that emotional engagement can require. He resisted for about a month, but one night when he was feeling particularly low he pressed the button and re-entered a world he thought he had left for ever.

The immediate results were devastating.

He was overwhelmed with a sense of shame and utter worthlessness. It took him a long time to come to see me, and by that time he was full of questions and gripped by doubts. It was hard work trying to convince him that Jesus still loved him and that he had not blown his chances of serving God in a meaningful way.

Men and women struggling in this area often confess a sense of utter worthlessness.

'How can God love me when I do such vile things?'

'I am a revolting human being – I cannot get the images I have seen out of my mind.'

'I hate myself. I've really blown it this time. God can never use me again.'

'I will never know the joy that I used to experience – it's gone for ever.'

'I'd love to find a wife, but I am so filthy that no woman would ever want me.'

'Am I even a Christian? Christians don't watch porn – I must be a sham. Was it ever real? Wouldn't it be better if I had never even tried to be a Christian in the first place?'

Flee from sexual immorality – letting God down

Sexual sin seems to have the capacity to produce the deepest and most profound sense of shame of all. Perhaps it is because sex was designed by God as the ultimate physical expression of the deepest emotions we can feel when we enter the most intense and intimate relationship that God has created – that between a husband and wife. There is something savage and dangerous about sex, and the only truly safe place for its expression is within the lifelong covenant relationship between one man and one woman in marriage. This is why Paul counsels us, 'Flee from sexual immorality. All other sins a person commits are outside the body, but whoever sins sexually, sins against their own body' (1 Corinthians 6:18).

It is not the role of this book to explore the way in which, as Christians, we can know increasing deliverance from pornography. There are already some excellent books out there that will help you think this through.[1] All I want to say here is that it is not enough just to demand self-discipline and practise self-control, good though these things are. We need to grasp the wonder of God's plans for us and to be captivated by the beauty of Christ. Only the power of the resurrection life of Christ will come anywhere near to combatting an addiction to porn.

Of course, the sense of shame that sin brings is not confined to sexual sin alone, although sexual sin is one of the most devastating disappointments that we can ever face. We want to serve God, and failure here can often lead to disenchantment, disillusionment and even despair.

Yes, we know that our status before God depends on the merits of Jesus rather than our own righteousness. Our justification is a declaration based on the finished work of Christ. Nonetheless, our self-image is tied up with the way in which we perceive ourselves and the level of our obedience to Christ and our conformity to his will.

It therefore matters when we feel that we have let God down, in the above area and more generally, and failed to please him. So,

- 'How do I cope with the guilt I feel about my broken marriage? I was in it for life. I never thought this would happen to me.'
- 'I know that God was calling me to ministry, but I wasn't willing to make the sacrifice. Now my life is just second best.'
- 'I was so young when I had the abortion, and I didn't really know what I was doing. But now I cannot get it out of my head. I know that God can never forgive me.'

- 'I don't mean to lose my temper, but when I do, I always hurt the people I love most. Once the words are out, I can't ever take them back.'
- 'I have never been unfaithful with another person, but I have let my wife down so badly. When she needs me, I am never there.'

Guilt and shame

Guilt and shame go hand in hand.

Guilt is the objective state when we have committed an offence that violates a law. It implies being responsible for an offence or a wrongdoing. It exists when we have done something forbidden, or failed to do something that was required. Shame, by contrast, is the subjective feeling that flows from the objective state of guilt. It is the painful consciousness that we have done something that is morally reprehensible.

We are hard-wired with a sense of right and wrong.

It is often the most 'moral' people who are most keenly aware of their own capacity for evil. Dag Hammarskjöld was Secretary General of the United Nations from 1953 to 1961. He was described as 'a great, good and lovable man'. But in his auto-biography *Markings*, he wrote of 'that dark counter-center of evil in our nature', which means that even our service for others is 'the foundation for our own life-preserving self-esteem'.[2]

One of the most disappointing things that we discover as Christians is that we are still incredibly flawed human beings who must struggle with imperfection, failure and sin.

The way ahead

So how do we deal with the debilitating effects of failure? What do we do when we are severely disappointed with ourselves?

Here are seven things:

- *Be clear about false guilt.* We all suffer from phantom guilt on occasions. This is a sense of shame that is not based on objective guilt. It may be satanic in origin – the devil delights in condemning God's people. Alternatively, it may be the result of an over-sensitive conscience or exposure to an unbalanced Bible ministry which emphasizes law and has little place for grace. We can easily mistake it for humility. In fact, it can flow from an unhealthy self-preoccupation, which is rooted in what we think we ought to be. It is an expression of pride rather than a fruit of meekness. Refuse to wallow in false guilt.
- *Be honest about real guilt.* The human heart is deceptive, and the Bible warns about the 'seared conscience' (1 Timothy 4:2). We therefore need to look hard and long at our sins and treat them with the gravity that they demand. We must neither minimize the sin nor blame someone else. This, of course, was the ploy of our first parents (Genesis 3). The Bible is clear:

> Whoever covers their sins does not prosper,
>   but the one who confesses and renounces them
>   finds mercy.
> (Proverbs 28:13)

- *Recognize that the battle with sin is lifelong.* There is no quick fix. Jesus taught his disciples to pray for forgiveness every day (Matthew 6:9–13). There is no final victory over sin in this life. We dwell in the interval between the first and second coming of Jesus. In this current world we will experience sickness, doubt and heartbreak. We will also need forgiveness every day if we are to complete the journey – anything else is self-deception (1 John 1:8–10).

- *Learn to hate sin for what it is, not just for its effects.* One of the problems in the battle with sin is that we concentrate more on the shame it brings, which we can feel, than the breach it makes in our relationship with God. Feelings of shame cause us to concentrate on the wrong element. What really matters is the honour of God, not my discomfort and unhappiness. The root of the problem is not how I feel, but objective guilt. John Bunyan once compared sin to the actions of those who punched Christ in the face at his trial:

> No sin against God can be little, because it is against the great God of heaven and earth; but if the sinner can find out a little God, it may be easy to find out little sins. Sin turns all God's grace into wantonness; it is the dare of his justice, the rape of his mercy, the jeer of his patience, the slight of his power, and the contempt of his love.[3]

- *Realize that your status before God depends on his grace, not your efforts.* When I fail, as I will, God's answer remains the same as ever: 'If we confess our sins, he is faithful and just and will forgive us our sins and purify us from all unrighteousness' (1 John 1:9). Jesus is the friend of sinners who never loses patience when we return from the dark paths of sin. In Christ we are set free from guilt and shame. While there may be consequences for our sin, the grace and the efficacy of the blood of Christ is enough for all our sins – past, present and future. Justification by faith is the gloriously liberating truth that I am righteous before God based on the imputed righteousness of Christ alone. So when God looks at me, he sees me in Christ. There is nothing more I can do to earn his favour, and there is nothing I will do that will forfeit it.

I find comfort in the words of Micah:

Who is a God like you,
>who pardons sin and forgives the transgression
>of the remnant of his inheritance?
You do not stay angry for ever
>but delight to show mercy.
You will again have compassion on us;
>you will tread our sins underfoot
>and hurl all our iniquities into the depths of the sea.
(Micah 7:18–19)

- *Recognize that holiness does matter.* So our status before God is based on the work of Christ, not our merits or obedience. However, holiness is not an optional extra reserved for a special class of Christian converts; it is the reason why God redeemed us in the first place. The happy life is the holy life. Once adopted into God's family, we will never lose our status as his children. He is not in the habit of tearing up our adoption papers. However, we can displease our Father, and this should matter to us. If we persist in sin, he will chasten us, and this will be a painful experience that we should seek to avoid. Remember Paul's prayer for the Colossians: 'We continually ask God to fill you with the knowledge of his will through all the wisdom and understanding that the Spirit gives, so that you may live a life worthy of the Lord and please him in every way' (Colossians 1:9–10).
- *Look forward to heaven when sin will no longer be a problem.* If you feel the weight of guilt and are depressed by the burden of sin, you are in good company. This is how Paul felt:

>So I find this law at work: although I want to do good, evil is right there with me. For in my inner being I delight in God's

law; but I see another law at work in me, waging war against
the law of my mind and making me a prisoner of the law
of sin at work within me. What a wretched man I am!
Who will rescue me from this body that is subject to death?
(Romans 7:21–24)

One of the joys of heaven will be the final deliverance from
the presence and power of sin that currently hem us in so
tightly.

A way back to God from the dark paths of sin

King David experienced the massive weight of guilt after his sin
with Bathsheba. A careless look leads to unquenched lust, which,
in turn, prepares the way for sexual sin, malicious deception and
premeditated murder. When David finally comes to his senses,
he appeals for mercy and, through having to live with consequences of failure, comes to taste the amazing grace of God.
He writes of this in Psalm 32:

Blessed is the one
    whose transgressions are forgiven,
    whose sins are covered.
Blessed is the one
    whose sin the LORD does not count against them
    and in whose spirit is no deceit.
(Psalm 32:1–2)

There is a wonderful vocabulary of forgiveness here. The word
'forgive' means to lift up or to lift off or to carry away. God
deliberately takes the burden off our shoulders and removes its
weight from us. Again, David writes that our sin is 'covered'. Sin
is blotted out or painted over. The ugly graffiti of iniquity is
never seen again, no longer counted against us. In the court of

divine justice there is no record. We have a clean slate, a fresh start. Whoever you are, whatever you may have done, there is grace with God, if you seek it.

David had learned a lot from his experience of grace, and he wants to share it with us. Deal with sin and guilt quickly – don't allow them to fester. If we ignore them, we will experience unnecessary grief. There is nothing more miserable than a Christian who is limping along with the weight of unacknowledged guilt:

> When I kept silent,
>> my bones wasted away
>> through my groaning all day long.
> For day and night
>> your hand was heavy on me;
> my strength was sapped
>> as in the heat of summer.
> (32:3–4)

The answer is confession:

> Then I acknowledged my sin to you
>> and did not cover up my iniquity.
> I said, 'I will confess
>> my transgressions to the LORD.'
> And you forgave
>> the guilt of my sin.
> (32:5)

It is important that we learn from David's experience. When the waters of guilt rise and threaten to engulf you, turn to the Lord and you will find him to be your stronghold:

> Therefore let all the faithful pray to you
>> while you may be found;

surely the rising of the mighty waters
    will not reach them.
You are my hiding-place;
    you will protect me from trouble
    and surround me with songs of deliverance.
(32:6–7)

Those who have experienced God's grace want to share it with others. Turn your disappointment into advice and testimony:

I will instruct you and teach you in the way you
        should go;
    I will counsel you with my loving eye on you.
Do not be like the horse or the mule,
    which have no understanding
but must be controlled by bit and bridle
    or they will not come to you.
Many are the woes of the wicked,
    but the LORD's unfailing love
    surrounds the one who trusts in him.
(32:8–10)

And the outcome? It will be wonder and amazement that God could forgive, and give you an upright heart:

Rejoice in the LORD and be glad, you righteous;
    sing, all you who are upright in heart!
(32:11)

Failure is not final

One of the most comforting truths in the Bible is that failure is not final. God forgives us, picks up the shattered fragments of our lives and continues to use us for his glory.

Consider two examples – one from each Testament.

Moses grew up as a prince in Egypt. At forty he attempted to liberate the people of Israel from oppression. It led to disaster and exile (Exodus 2). It seemed as if God had sidelined him. For forty years he kept sheep in the desert of Midian. Did he grieve over his wasted education and training? Was he gripped by a sense of lost opportunity?

But when Moses was eighty God spoke to him at the burning bush and called him to return to Egypt and liberate the people. This was God's time. Moses' reluctance is born out of a sense of humility. Disappointment has taught him not to trust himself and his own resources. But in this condition God takes him up and uses him to bring about the salvation of the nation:

> But Moses said to God, 'Who am I that I should go to Pharaoh and bring the Israelites out of Egypt?'
>
> And God said, 'I will be with you. And this will be the sign to you that it is I who have sent you: when you have brought the people out of Egypt, you will worship God on this mountain.'
>
> Moses said to God, 'Suppose I go to the Israelites and say to them, "The God of your fathers has sent me to you," and they ask me, "What is his name?" Then what shall I tell them?'
>
> God said to Moses, 'I AM WHO I AM. This is what you are to say to the Israelites: "I am has sent me to you."'
> (Exodus 3:11–14)

This giving of the divine name is both a revelation of mystery and an invitation to intimacy. Moses, the failure, knows God's name and can speak on his behalf. Disappointment at personal failure has shaped him so that God can use him. The Bible later says of him, 'Now Moses was a very humble man, more humble than anyone else on the face of the earth' (Numbers 12:3).

When you consider all that God revealed to him and all that God did through him, this is a remarkable statement. Moses learned that failure does not disqualify you for service, and God delights in using flawed people. Failure is not final.

Our second example is Peter. In the best-documented public failure in the history of the church, Peter denied the Lord three times. It was compounded by the fact that Jesus had warned him, so Peter should have known better. It occurred when Jesus seemed to be at his most vulnerable. Luke alone records one of the most poignant details of the event:

> Peter replied, 'Man, I don't know what you're talking about!' Just as he was speaking, the cock crowed. The Lord turned and looked straight at Peter. Then Peter remembered the word the Lord had spoken to him: 'Before the cock crows today, you will disown me three times.' And he went outside and wept bitterly. (Luke 22:60–62)

Can you feel the pathos here? Jesus has been beaten and he probably has the spit of the soldiers running down his face. At this point he locks eyes with Peter. What shame did Peter feel? What anguish gripped his heart? It is no wonder that Luke tells us that Peter went out and wept bitterly.

These are the tears of anguished disappointment. How could he have let his Master down so badly? Three years of preparation for leadership have gone up in smoke. He will never lead the church as Jesus had intended.

But we know the end of the story. Three days later the risen Christ appears to Peter on his own, and then to Peter and the apostles (Luke 24:33–49; John 20:19–23). His first words are not 'Shame on you', but 'Peace be with you.' Some time later Jesus prepares breakfast on the beach for them and he reinstates Peter, commanding him to care for his flock (John 21:1–23). And fifty days after the resurrection Peter is boldly proclaiming the gospel to crowds in the city of Jerusalem (Acts 2:14–39).

This is in fulfilment of what Jesus predicted on the night of his betrayal: 'Simon, Simon, Satan has asked to sift all of you as wheat. But I have prayed for you, Simon, that your faith may not fail. And when you have turned back, strengthen your brothers' (Luke 22:31–32).

Jesus knew the worst about (Simon) Peter, but he still loved him and prayed for him. His intention was always that afterwards Peter would be restored and exercise many years of fruitful ministry.

Jesus knows the worst about us, but he still loves us and prays for us. His intention is always to restore those who have failed.

Failure is not final. God does not want you to remember what he has chosen to forget.

Questions

1. How does the devil use guilt and shame to paralyse Christians?
2. How do we distinguish between real guilt and phantom guilt?
3. What are the main steps to overcoming an addiction to pornography? Where can we look for help? Are we prepared to deal decisively with it?
4. Begin to make a list of verses that you might turn to when you feel guilty.
5. Work through Psalm 32. How does it help us to deal with the disappointment of failure?

9. 'I'm the only one left, and they are trying to kill me': when even God seems to let us down

The story is told of a young minister who wanted to impress a congregation with his grasp of the Bible. So one Sunday morning he announced that he was going to preach through the whole of the Old Testament in one sermon.

'Let us begin at the beginning. God created everything out of nothing.' He launched forth.

He proceeded to outline the well-known stories contained in the opening chapters of Genesis. He moved from Adam and Eve to Cain and Abel, Noah, Abraham and the family he established. By now, he had been going for some time, but was building a head of steam and felt confident that his hitherto uncomplaining congregation was with him. He preached about Moses and the exodus, Joshua and the conquest, the difficult days of the Judges, the glory days of David and the magnificence of Solomon. He was well past the hour mark, but oblivious to the fidgeting of the congregation.

'So now we come to the sad days of the divided kingdom and the ministry of Elijah. Oh, what a great man he was! What shall we do with Elijah? Where shall we put Elijah?' he asked, with dramatic flourish.

At this point a voice called from the back of the auditorium, 'He can have my seat. I'm going home for my dinner.'

It is not recorded whether or not the minister finished his sermon.

A good question

But it is a good question. Where indeed shall we put Elijah?

He is one of the most towering figures of the Old Testament. If Moses was the great lawgiver, then Elijah was the great defender of the law. It is the ninth century BC, and the political and religious regime in Israel is attempting to replace the worship of Yahweh with the worship of Baal. It has been orchestrated by King Ahab, spurred on by the sinister machinations of Jezebel, his pagan wife. It looks as if evil is triumphing as those who are faithful to God go into hiding or are murdered. The countryside is littered with pagan shrines, vile images, sacred prostitution and child sacrifice. Contempt exists for God and his word. It is as if Satan himself had taken up residence in Israel, and the country is being polluted with the raw sewage of evil (1 Kings 16:21–28).

And then, suddenly, out of nowhere comes Elijah. He appears in the court and confronts the king. It is not Baal who sends the rain that secures the fertility of the land; it is Yahweh. There will therefore be no rain until this is acknowledged (1 Kings 17:1). After a three-year drought the nation gathers on the top of Mount Carmel, and God proves that he alone is the living God – the God who answers with fire (1 Kings 18:16–40). The people bow to the supremacy of Yahweh, and the rain falls (1 Kings 18:41–46). Shortly after this, Elijah appoints Elisha to complete the task of removing the cancer of Baalism from the land. There are further confrontations with Ahab, and then Elijah is taken up to heaven in a whirlwind.

The Old Testament ends with the promise of a future prophet like Elijah who will prepare the way for the Messiah

(Malachi 4:5–6). Jesus acknowledges that it is John the Baptist who fulfils this role (Matthew 11:14).

So where shall we put Elijah? The answer must be right up there with other great examples of courageous faith in the Bible.

And yet . . .

And yet, we have skirted around one of the most enigmatic incidents in the Bible – the moment when Elijah's disappointment with God was so great that his faith seemed to buckle under the weight.

The story is well known. Elijah has experienced God's miraculous protection for three years. This has been followed by God's supernatural vindication of his name at Mount Carmel. The first result of this is national public repentance:

> Then the fire of the LORD fell and burned up the sacrifice,
> the wood, the stones and the soil, and also licked up the water
> in the trench.
>   When all the people saw this, they fell prostrate and cried,
> 'The LORD – he is God! The LORD – he is God!'
> (1 Kings 18:38–39)

The second result is that those responsible for the foul religion of Baal are removed:

> Then Elijah commanded them, 'Seize the prophets of Baal.
> Don't let anyone get away!' They seized them, and Elijah had
> them brought down to the Kishon Valley and slaughtered there.
> (1 Kings 18:40)

And then the rain comes – a sure sign of God's forgiveness and mercy for a repentant nation.

At this point it must have seemed that Elijah's hopes and dreams had been realized. Baalism was dead and buried. The king would repent of his evil ways. Jezebel would be removed. The nation would return to wholehearted allegiance to Yahweh.

But Jezebel had other ideas:

> Now Ahab told Jezebel everything Elijah had done and how he had killed all the prophets with the sword. So Jezebel sent a messenger to Elijah to say, 'May the gods deal with me, be it ever so severely, if by this time tomorrow I do not make your life like that of one of them.'
>
> (1 Kings 19:1–2)

The resilience of evil

It is interesting to notice in passing the resilience of evil.

Jezebel is a symbol of those who persistently and vindictively oppose the people of God. Throughout the history of the church, and right up to the present day, this opposition continues. Totalitarian systems cannot accept any allegiance that is higher than that demanded by the regime. For most of us, the opposition is less brutal but just as spiteful.

Behind this we see the malicious and malevolent hand of the devil. We are opposed by a powerful, cunning and determined foe. Christ may have struck the decisive blow against him, but although he is beaten, he will not lie down. Paul warns us that behind the disappointments that we face – in church, in the world and in the home – are the slimy manoeuvrings of spiritual forces of evil (Ephesians 6:10–20).

We must not mistake one victory for the end of the war. Every triumph is only partial. After their failure to assassinate members of the British government by bombing the Grand Hotel in Brighton in 1984, the IRA issued this chilling warning: 'Today we were unlucky, but remember we only have to be lucky once. You will have to be lucky always.'[1]

It is naive to think that there will ever be an armistice while we are still on this earth. God will finally deal with the devil at the end of the age. Until then we will never live in a devil-free zone. And one of his chief weapons is discouragement. If unchecked, this can lead to disillusionment, depression and despair. We would be foolish to think that we are immune to such attacks. Many things can transform disappointment into despair, but Satan often has a hand in the process.

The consistent biblical defence against the devil is to stand firm and meet his lies with the truth of Scripture. Paul speaks of the belt of truth and the sword of the Spirit which is the word of God (Ephesians 6:14, 17). Disappointment feeds on falsehood. Faith meets fabrication with fact. We choose to believe what God says in the objective truths of Scripture, rather than succumbing to Satan's seductive slanders.

The mountain of despair

From what we already know of Elijah, we may expect him to take this new hurdle in his stride.

But it leads to the great crisis of his life:

> Elijah was afraid and ran for his life. When he came to Beersheba in Judah, he left his servant there, while he himself went a day's journey into the wilderness. He came to a broom bush, sat down under it and prayed that he might die. 'I have had enough, LORD,' he said. 'Take my life; I am no better than my ancestors.' Then he lay down under the bush and fell asleep.
> (1 Kings 19:3–5)

Much has been written to explain the apparent collapse of Elijah's faith. He often gets a bad press. Was he exhausted by the events of the previous months? Was he so full of his own sense of achievement that he took his eyes off God? Is this an example of pride coming before a fall? Should he have known better? Is this an example of the long-term results of stress? Is he having a nervous breakdown? Is he suffering from terminal loneliness? Has fear replaced faith so that all he can think to do is to run away to safety? Has this volcano of a man become a damp squib?

There may be truth in some of these suggestions, but I think that they miss the point. What is clear is that he had a crisis of faith. This was brought on by disappointment, and he was in danger of despair. Seeing no way out, he prayed to die.

But what was the nature of the disappointment?

The above passage gives us several clues.

Look again at his actions. Elijah ran for his life. We cannot blame him for this. Sometimes discretion is the better part of valour. It would have been foolish to throw his life away when there was still work to do. But when we check the geography, we discover that more than discretion is at work here. He runs to Beersheba, which is in the extreme south of Judah. It is about as far away from Jezebel as he can get. At this point he is physically safe from her revenge. But he does not stay there. After a restorative meal and refreshing sleep, he moves on to Mount Horeb, the place where the law was given and God made a covenant with his people. He is not fleeing from danger, but fleeing to God. He is not running from Jezebel; he is running into the arms of his Father. He has been defending and applying the covenant. It is the covenant that Ahab has broken. So he is returning to the place where the covenant was made in the first place. And what he does when he gets there is remind God of what he had promised. The covenant had stipulated that those who broke it would be punished by God. This has happened to a certain extent, but Baalism continues to flourish. Why has God not kept his word to eradicate evil?

Disappointed because we care

It is in this context that we can understand Elijah's repeated complaint:

> I have been very zealous for the LORD God Almighty. The
> Israelites have rejected your covenant, torn down your altars,
> and put your prophets to death with the sword. I am the only
> one left, and now they are trying to kill me too.
> (1 Kings 19:10, 14)

This is not the whinging of a self-absorbed man. Nor is it an egotistical little pity party. It is, rather, the lament of a man who has given everything for God's glory and honour and is now disappointed that his efforts seem to have failed. He is disappointed because he is passionate for the cause of truth. It is his zeal for God and his honour that has shattered him and brought him to despair. God had said that he would punish his enemies, but instead they are rampant. He had said that he would protect his people, but instead they are perishing. He had promised that he would defend his honour, but now it is being despised.

Elijah is a man on fire.

We are reminded of the words of Bishop Ryle:

> A zealous man in religion is pre-eminently a man of one thing.
> It is not enough to say that he is earnest, hearty, uncompromising,
> thorough-going, whole-hearted, fervent in spirit. He sees one
> thing, he cares for one thing, he lives for one thing, he is
> swallowed up in one thing – and that one thing is to please
> God. Whether he lives – or whether he dies; whether he has
> health – or whether he has sickness; whether he is rich – or
> whether he is poor; whether he pleases man – or whether he
> gives offence; whether he is thought wise – or whether he is
> thought foolish; whether he gets blame – or whether he gets

praise; whether he gets honour, or whether he gets shame – for
all this the zealous man cares nothing at all. He burns for one
thing – and that one thing is to please God, and to advance
God's glory.[2]

And it is this burning zeal for God's glory that explains the depths
of his disappointment. Christianity is not meant to be cool and
dispassionate. We are supposed to love God and his honour. And
this very thing will make us vulnerable. How often do we feel
the smart of disappointment because we love Jesus and are
concerned that others do not share this love? We invite someone
to the carol service, but we are turned down. We witness to a
neighbour or work colleague, only to be told that they think our
most cherished beliefs are just plain stupid. We work hard
teaching in Sunday school or youth group, only to find that the
kids reject Jesus and walk away. We labour in pastoral ministry,
but see so little fruit. We read the statistics of unbelief and are
shocked by the small number of real Christians in our nation.
We are shaken at the advance of secularism, not so much that
people have a worked-out atheism, just that they do not see the
relevance of faith and are contemptuous of the idea that God
might have any authority over their lives. We get disappointed
because we care.

Disappointment is one of the occupational hazards of evangel-
ists! We know that there is a clear demarcation of responsibilities
– one sows and another reaps, but only God gives the increase
(1 Corinthians 3:6). We are clear that our job is to give a reason
for the hope that is in us, and that only God can open blind eyes
and breathe life into dead souls. But so much is at stake that we
cannot be dispassionate when our friends reject the gospel.
We pay a price for love. Paul paid this price:

I speak the truth in Christ – I am not lying, my conscience
confirms it through the Holy Spirit – I have great sorrow and
unceasing anguish in my heart. For I could wish that I myself

were cursed and cut off from Christ for the sake of my people,
those of my own race, the people of Israel.
(Romans 9:1–4)

So did Elijah.

The mountain of hope

There may be some practical lessons that we can learn from this
story. Perhaps Elijah had foolishly neglected the rhythms of life.
We too need to rest and to unwind. There is no merit in burning
out by neglecting the biblical principles of work, rest and play.
Surely it is significant that the angel gives Elijah food and sleep,
and then more food before the journey to Horeb (1 Kings 19:5–9).
We do not live by bread alone, but it certainly helps.

But clearly, the most significant emphasis in the story is the
way in which God comes to meet with his servant. What strikes
us is how gentle, and yet firm, he is. He does not rebuke Elijah,
but he reveals himself to his servant and recommissions him for
the next phase of his ministry. God is much kinder than we are.
He is slow to anger and he remembers that we are dust (Psalm
103:8–18).

The restoration of Elijah involves a vision and a voice.

First, the vision: God reveals himself to the prophet (19:11–13).
After a cosmic firework display which overwhelms the senses,
God affirms that he is not in the wind or the earthquake or the
fire. Of course, God is sometimes revealed in such phenomena – it was here at Horeb / Sinai that he had appeared in fire
(Exodus 19). But he is not confined to the spectacular. On this
occasion his presence is seen and felt in a 'still small voice'.

What does this mean?

God can 'do' the spectacular if he wants to. The events
of Carmel were spectacular. So was the crossing of the Red Sea
and the fall of Jericho. When God pours out his Spirit and there

is revival, remarkable and unprecedented things do happen (Acts 2:1–4).

But it is a mistake to think that if we do not see extravagant results, God is not at work. Sometimes God works quietly and in an unseen way – like the leaven that is gently but invincibly permeating the dough (Matthew 13:33). Remember back in chapter 4 where we looked at the seed growing secretly (Mark 4:26–29)? We don't need to keep pulling it up and checking the roots. God is working even when we do not see it. The message is clear. Don't get discouraged by the lack of fruit. It's only natural to be disappointed when you feel passionately about the honour of God. But you can leave it to God to build his kingdom. It's his call, not yours. Do your duty and do it joyfully, and then leave the results with God. And whatever the results look like – amazingly spectacular or decidedly mundane – you can trust God. Never underestimate the gentle whisper of God's powerful, saving and Christ-exalting word.

And after the vision comes the voice.

God gives three assurances that reinforce what Elijah has been learning.

First, God has a plan (19:15–17). He will punish his enemies and purge Baalism from the nation's life. In doing this, he will employ the secular forces of history to do his bidding, including Hazael king of Syria and Jehu the future king of Israel. They will destroy Ahab's dynasty and replace him as king (see 2 Kings 9 – 10). The sovereign God does not look out on the world with helpless impotence. He reigns, and his purposes will not fail. We may appear to lose a battle, but we will one day win the war. Disappointed prophets and discouraged people are reassured when they hear this.

Second, God has a man (19:17). Elijah had lamented that there was no-one left (19:14). God assures him that he already has his replacement lined up! Elisha is waiting in the wings and he will complete the work that Elijah began. We need to learn a vitally important lesson from this. God removes his servants but continues his work. We are right to be passionate for his cause, but no-one is indispensable. We may fail, but God will succeed. God is the real hero of the story and he will not share that glory with anyone else.

Finally, God has a people (19:18). There is a faithful remnant who have not succumbed to false religion, but have been faithful to Yahweh. God will always have a people in the world. Jesus will build his church, and the gates of hell will not prevail against it (Matthew 16:18).

And so Elijah returns to the fight – refreshed, restored and recommissioned.

We can easily become discouraged in our ministry. But in the end, it is God's cause and he will see it through. If we care, disappointments will smart. This is part of the cost of Christian service. Like Elijah, we can be honest with God and tell him how we feel. And like Elijah, we can find reassurance in the tender reproof of a God who will certainly complete the work he has called us to be part of. We can rise above such disappointments and endure to the end.

Be inspired by the words of the apostle Paul:

> But we have this treasure in jars of clay to show that this all-surpassing power is from God and not from us. We are hard pressed on every side, but not crushed; perplexed, but not in despair; persecuted, but not abandoned; struck down, but not destroyed. We always carry around in our body the death of Jesus, so that the life of Jesus may also be revealed in our body. (2 Corinthians 4:7–10)

Questions

1. The Bible is full of people who expressed their disappointment with God. What examples can you think of?

2. Elijah's experience is very like that of the prophet Habakkuk. Look up the Old Testament book of Habakkuk:

   - What was Habakkuk's first complaint and God's reply (1:1–11)?
   - What was Habakkuk's second complaint and how did God reply this time (1:12 – 2:20)?
   - What did Habakkuk pray and how did he express his faith (3:1–19)?

3. How can we be zealous for God without experiencing burnout?
4. If you feel discouraged at the moment, what do you need in order to return to the fight refreshed, restored and recommissioned?

The power that preserves

10. His name is Toby: God is good

'I was with my son his entire life. Two minutes.'

In a moving account, Marshall Shelley, one of the editors of *Christianity Today*, tells the story of the death of his son. During the pregnancy Marshall and his wife Susan had learned that their child had a heart abnormality and probably would not survive birth. They prayed, however, that their boy would survive the pregnancy, and that God would give them some time with their son.

Their prayer was answered, and he was born at 8:20 p.m. on 22 November 1991.

He was a healthy pink colour, and Mum and Dad rejoiced to see his chest rise and fall with the breath of life. But within seconds he turned from pink to blue, and at 8:22 p.m. he died. The mystery of life quickly gave way to the tragedy of death.

When the nurse tenderly asked the Shelleys if they had a name for the child, Susan replied, 'Toby. It's short for the biblical name, Tobiah, which means "God is good".'[1]

Marshall poignantly writes,

My wife, Susan, and I never got to see him take his first steps. We barely got to see him take his first breath. I don't know if he would have enjoyed softball or software, dinosaurs or dragonflies, machines or math. We never got to wrestle, race, or read – would he have enjoyed those things like his older sisters do? What would have made him laugh? Made him scared? Made him angry?[2]

And yet he wants to affirm the goodness of God.

He continues,

The words of C. S. Lewis, describing the lion Aslan, kept coming to mind: 'He's not a tame lion. But he's good.' We clung to that image of untamed and fearsome goodness, even as we continued to struggle with the question: Why would God create a child to live two minutes?[3]

He reflected that in those two minutes, it was as if eternity intersected with time. Toby was created for eternity. Two minutes on earth do not represent the end of the story. Marshall and Susan are convinced that Toby will have an eternal existence.

We can only affirm the goodness of God from this eternal perspective.

On our journey through the Land of Disappointment we have visited some painful places – places that may be familiar to many of us.

In this next part of our journey we will turn away from specific areas of disappointment and focus our attention on some of the great and abiding certainties of the Christian faith. These truths give us the power to persevere and keep going, even when we feel like giving up. It is God's powerful grip on our lives that preserves us to the end of the journey.

We begin with the glorious truth of the unequivocal goodness of God.

Groaning in pain

Romans 8, which we looked at earlier, is the capstone of Paul's great statement of the gospel of justification by faith alone.

Here he works out some of the implications of this salvation. It contains both sublime theology and awesome pastoral insight.

Like the author of Ecclesiastes, Paul knows that the world is broken and that being a believer does not protect us from disappointment and distress. Our current experience is binary: we know both discomfort and confidence.

This twofold experience is summarized in two very similar statements at the heart of the chapter.

Take the discomfort first:

> We know that the whole creation has been groaning as in the pains of childbirth right up to the present time. Not only so, but we ourselves, who have the firstfruits of the Spirit, groan inwardly as we wait eagerly for our adoption to sonship, the redemption of our bodies.
>
> (Romans 8:22–23)

The experience of childbirth is both intensely painful and immensely fruitful. Pain is the portal to life. The creation groans because it has not yet reached all that God will one day make it. It is poised between decay and glory. As Christians, we have tasted something of this glory to come – we know that God is our Father, Jesus is our brother and the Holy Spirit has sealed our hearts for the day of redemption. We have peace about the past, purpose in the present and confidence for the future. At the same time we groan inwardly as we struggle with sin, decay and doubt. We experience the 'trapeze anxiety' that we discovered in chapter 1.

This will not end until we receive new bodies at the resurrection.

Here is the answer to those who try to persuade us that if we do not enjoy health, wealth and prosperity, we are somehow living beneath our privileges. God has the whole of eternity to make up for all the pains of this world, but while we are in the present body, our experience is poised between the 'already' and the 'not yet'.

And this is very confusing. We often do not know how to pray:

> In the same way, the Spirit helps us in our weakness. We do not know what we ought to pray for, but the Spirit himself intercedes for us through wordless groans. And he who searches our hearts knows the mind of the Spirit, because the Spirit intercedes for God's people in accordance with the will of God.
> (8:26–27)

Beneath our groaning is the mystery of God groaning – the wonder of God praying to God. I am reminded of a visit to one of my friends in a hospital ward. Terry was an articulate and strong-minded Yorkshireman. He would quip, 'You can always tell a Yorkshireman, but you can't tell him much.'

Now a series of strokes has reduced his ability to communicate. His wife Joan sits next to the bed, gripping his hand tightly and smiling warmly at the man she loves. I feel as if I am trespassing on holy ground, but the moment they become aware of my presence Terry tries to speak and Joan moves even closer to catch the words. To me they seem incoherent and unintelligible. But not to Joan. 'He says he is pleased to see you, pastor. Will you read the Bible for us?'

In the same way the Holy Spirit takes our clumsy, faltering prayers which flow from hearts full of pain and makes them eloquent in heaven.

What we know

But that is not the whole story.

Immediately after confessing that we know that we are part of a creaking creation, Paul tells us something else that we know:

> And we know that in all things God works for the good of those who love him, who have been called according to his purpose.

For those God foreknew he also predestined to be conformed
to the image of his Son, that he might be the firstborn among
many brothers and sisters. And those he predestined, he also
called; those he called, he also justified; those he justified, he
also glorified.
(8:28–30)

These words are the softest pillow on which many a disappointed
saint has come to rest a weary head. Here Paul articulates the
great truth of Christian providence. God governs all things with
wisdom, love and care. This is not a vague feeling or a longed-for
possibility. It is a deep-seated conviction.

Paul's statement contains three things: an affirmation (8:28),
an explanation (8:29) and a confirmation (8:29–30).

An affirmation

Behind the events of this life is the steadying hand of God,
our Father. Paul wants to affirm that 'God works all things for
good'. It is not fate or chance or Mother Nature, but the hand
of the God and Father of our Lord Jesus Christ. There is a personal God who shapes all events in our lives. And we know him
personally – we have a friend behind the phenomena. There is
a script that our lives follow, and each paragraph and sentence
and word is inscribed by an author who loves us and plans good
for us.

Notice that Paul is convinced that this involves 'all' things. His
vision is comprehensive. It covers prosperity and adversity,
sickness and health, joys and sorrows, blessings and trials – the
good and the bad and the ugly. In God's universe there is not a
single maverick molecule that can refuse his direction or derail
his purposes. This includes those painful and disappointing
occurrences that conspire to confuse us. The God of the Bible
is not an impotent observer looking at a world out of control
and wringing his hands with helplessness. He is the sovereign
Lord in heaven who does what pleases him (Psalm 115:3).

There is, of course, a great mystery here: we are free agents who make real decisions that count. We are not robots or puppets on a string. On the other hand, God works all things according to his will. As the missionary Amy Carmichael is reputed to have observed, he is never outmanoeuvred or taken by surprise. There is never a crisis or panic in heaven. God does not have problems; he has only plans.

And there is more, for this God works all things for our good. But here's the rub. Is Paul saying that pain and disappointment and even sin are good in themselves? Should I rejoice because of the things that distress me? Should I be grateful for agony and glad about grief? Should I encourage the elderly Christian woman who feels the chill of loss since the death of her husband – the only man she has ever loved – to thank God that he is no longer there to take her in his arms and kiss away her tears? Is Paul trying to persuade us that these things are good in and of themselves?

This would be a bizarre and an unbearable doctrine. How can I thank God for the death of my dad at the age of sixty or for the loss of my child or for the sin that still dogs my steps? And, of course, Paul is not asking me to do so. If these things are not good in themselves, then what does he mean?

It is the *purpose* that is good.

We can and should hate those things that distress us. When I find that in my absence my wife's lack of balance due to her MS has made her fall yet again, I am devastated. Naturally. Tell me to thank God for her bruises, and I will be less than polite!

What we can be sure of is that God has a purpose and is using the disappointments in life to accomplish something bigger and better. He can 'sanctify to us our deepest distress'.[4]

Imagine that I have a raging toothache that keeps me awake. In the end I visit the dentist because I can bear the pain no longer. He takes one look and tells me that the tooth must be removed. He straps me to the chair, clamps open my mouth and injects my gum with a nine-inch needle. When my mouth feels like a downy pillow, he approaches with a shining metal implement that would not look out of place in a medieval torture chamber. He then uses the device to extract the offending molar. I spit out blood and gum and broken tooth and he asks me how I feel.

'Wonderful. Please do it again – I've got another thirty-one to go.'

Of course not!

But when I get home and the anaesthetic wears off, I discover that the pain is gone. For the first time in weeks I am able to sleep. The process was painful, but the purpose was good. And this is what Paul means. We are not supposed to delight in distress and revel in regrets. But we can be certain that God's purpose is always good: 'Not one detail works ultimately for evil to the people of God. In the end only good will be their lot.'[5]

But before we leave this, notice that it is not a general promise for all people. It is a specific promise of a specific purpose for a specific people. They are defined as 'those who love [God], who have been called according to his purpose'. It is a promise to those who love God because they have experienced his grace and been reconciled by the blood of his Son.

An explanation

So what is God's purpose? Paul begins to explain it in the next verse. Through the pressure of painful and disappointing circumstances, God is patiently and deliberately moulding our lives so that we are being 'conformed to the image of his Son' (8:29).

Human beings were created in the image of God – both to resemble him and to represent him in the rule of his world (Genesis 1:26–28). After the sin of our first parents, that image was marred but not destroyed. There are still more than 7 billion image-bearers on planet earth, but the image is so badly disfigured that it is often almost impossible to discern. However, God has not abandoned his original project of creating a race of people who will act as his regents in the world he has made. First, he sent his Son as the perfect image of the invisible God (Colossians 1:15). Then he began the work of transformation, calling out individuals to be transformed into the likeness of Jesus. One day that work will be complete, and the original purpose – reigning with Christ over a restored cosmos – will be finished (1 John 3:1–2; Revelation 22:1–5). Christ is thus the firstborn of a whole family of men and women who will share his character and destiny.

At this moment we are living in the tension of what we are and what we will be. It is that painful season of character forming which the Bible calls 'sanctification', or being made holy. Like a master craftsman, God is working with the somewhat inferior materials of our lives in order to transform us into the likeness of his Son.

Between 1501 and 1504 Michelangelo worked on a five-metre-high piece of marble, which had been quarried forty years before. The sculptor Agostino di Duccio had begun to create a giant figure of one of the prophets, but abandoned the project as impossible. The marble lay neglected for ten years until Antonio Rossellino also made an attempt to use it, only to discard it as too difficult to work. He complained that it was poor quality and predicted that it would never be of any use.

Thirty years later Michelangelo found the abandoned piece of poor-quality marble and began his great project, creating perhaps his most famous work, the statue of David. This was his masterpiece. The sixteenth-century painter and architect Giorgio Vasari said of it, 'Whoever has seen this work need not trouble to see any other work executed in sculpture, either in our own or in other times.'[6]

Michelangelo took something that was rejected and useless, and created a stunning piece of art that has never ceased to impress the observer. We might say that he saw David beneath the surface of an inferior piece of stone. He then released him from the marble, using hammer and chisel to cut away everything that wasn't David.

In like manner, God takes us, fallen and inferior as we are, and seeks to recreate us in the image of his Son. Disappointment is just one of the tools that he employs to cut away everything that is not like Jesus. Paul has already affirmed this a few chapters earlier:

> We also glory in our sufferings, because we know that suffering produces perseverance; perseverance, character; and character, hope. And hope does not put us to shame, because God's love has been poured out into our hearts through the Holy Spirit, who has been given to us.
> (Romans 5:3–5)

The process may be painful – but the purpose is good.

A confirmation

But can we be certain?

Sometimes it feels very shallow and simplistic when people assure us that suffering is good for us. Those who speak by the yard and think by the inch deserve to be kicked by the foot! The Bible never does this – it takes our tears seriously. But it wants to assure us that this process is designed and executed by God, and that we can rest in the knowledge of his goodness and grace.

In Romans 8:29–30 Paul confirms what he has been saying by reminding us that God's plans reach from eternity to eternity, swooping down to lift us out of the mire of sin and preparing us for glory to come.

God foreknew us. This is not merely a factual knowledge. It is the relational knowledge of love. God set his heart on his people before the foundation of the world. He did not just see our faith and nudge us in the right direction. He loved us in eternity.

God predestined us. He chose us in Christ. I am a Christian not because I chose God, but because he chose me. This doctrine of election is difficult to grasp, and we often struggle with it.

However, it is not a banner to march under or a bomb to drop; it is a bastion to hide in. I am loved by God even though I do not deserve it. He knew the worst that there was to know about me and yet he still loved me and chose to send his Son to rescue me.

God called us. A day came when we heard the call of Christ and we fled to him for salvation. We came from darkness into light, from death to life, from the world to Christ, from sin to holiness and from self into God.

God justified us. He declared us righteous in his sight. It is not that he gave us a second chance to try to live better lives. He gave us the full package of salvation, so that we are ready to meet God's scrutiny on the Day of Judgment because he now sees us in Christ.

God glorifies us. This is the climax of the process, the moment when we receive the redemption of our bodies and are perfectly transformed to be like Jesus. There is no longer any need for God to use pain to shape us, because we will be made holy and blameless – finally transformed into the likeness of Jesus. In imperishable and perfect bodies we will reign with him for ever, sharing in God's own glory.

Romans 8:31–39 drives this home.

The process we are part of is sure of a perfect outcome. In John Stott's words, Paul wants to assure us that 'nothing can frustrate God's purpose . . . quench his generosity . . . or condemn his elect . . . or sunder us from his love'.[7]

'None of the ransomed ever knew'

My first pastor, Les Coley, taught me many things. He taught me to love God's word and to love his people. He taught me to preach. And he taught me that whenever we are faced with a dilemma – theological or pastoral or personal – we should always return to the cross. All our theology must be worked out within earshot of Calvary. The cross is the supreme demonstration of all God's attributes.

Can we really believe in the goodness of God?

The cross tells us that we can. Here is goodness incarnate and nailed to a wooden plank. Evidences of God's goodness are all around us, but there is absolutely nothing like this. We can never understand the magnitude of God's goodness until we stand in the shadow of the cross.

Crucifixion was the ultimate deterrent in the Roman Empire, designed to terrify the subdued people who might challenge its might. But the physical pain that Jesus experienced was only an external manifestation of the deeper suffering that swamped his soul as he descended into the darkness of judgment on Calvary. There was light and glory at midnight when Christ was born (Luke 2:8–14). At his death there was darkness at noon (Luke 23:44–45). For three hours the 'sun stopped shining'. God himself veils this solemn moment as the creation grieves at the death of the Creator. This is the darkness of judgment (Amos 8:9–10). God lays our sins on Christ and then punishes him as if he were personally responsible for all of them. At that moment he who knew no sin was made sin for us (2 Corinthians 5:21).

Out of the darkness Jesus cries out, '"*Eloi, Eloi, lema sabachthani?*" (which means "My God, my God, why have you forsaken me?")' (Mark 15:34).

These are the terrible torments of a condemned man. He stands where he has never stood before, enduring all the punishment that we deserve.

> But none of the ransomed ever knew
>> How deep were the waters crossed;
> Nor how dark was the night which the Lord passed through
>> Ere He found His sheep that was lost.[8]

So do we believe in the goodness of God? Can we be certain that God is really working all things for our good?

The cross gives us permission to do so. In the midst of disappointment it is easy to lose sight of God's purpose. We need to step back and recognize God's smile behind adversity:

The Lord is good and his mercy endures for ever;
    his faithfulness continues through all generations.
(Psalm 100:5)

Questions

1. Read again Toby's story at the head of this chapter. How does Marshall Shelley justify his affirmation of the goodness of God? What can we learn from this?
2. What evidence is there that this world is groaning in pain?
3. Read through Romans 8 and make a note of every reference to the Holy Spirit. How does the Holy Spirit help us?
4. How does God use disappointment to make us like Jesus? How can we invest our disappointments well?
5. The Puritan writer John Flavel said the following about God's use of suffering to mould our lives:

> Providence so orders the case, that faith and prayer come between our wants and supplies, and the goodness of God may be the more magnified in our eyes thereby.[9]

- How do faith and prayer come between our wants and God's supplies?
- How does adversity magnify the goodness of God?
- How does the cross give us permission to affirm the goodness of God?

11. The darling of heaven: Jesus is sufficient

One of the longest-running BBC series is the evergreen *Desert Island Discs*. First broadcast on 9 January 1942, there have been over 3,000 episodes at the time of writing. The guest or castaway is invited to choose eight recordings. At the conclusion of the programme they are allowed one luxury and one book, apart from the Bible and the complete works of Shakespeare.

If you have ever listened to the programme, you have probably tried to make your own selection. The last time I did so, I struggled to give sufficient place to Leonard Cohen, Bob Dylan, Johnny Cash and Tchaikovsky. Not easy! I've also had a go with favourite hymns and movies. However, my favourite exercise is to construct a list of eight books I would not want to be without. I've tried it both with Christian books and secular volumes. The list keeps changing. However, there is one book that has been a permanent fixture since I first discovered it: *The Glory of Christ* by the preacher-theologian Peter Lewis.

Peter writes warmly and penetratingly as he seeks to present Jesus Christ in all his glory and winsomeness. It is a mixture of mind-stretching theology and warm devotion, which engages our hearts and persuades us that all we could ever desire is to be found in Christ.

I was hooked from the opening illustration.

Peter shares a story told by a preacher he heard in his native Wales. When he was about twelve, this man idolized a local rugby player and plastered his bedroom walls with newspaper clippings and photos recording the great man's exploits. The preacher takes up the story:

> When I was fourteen, I got to know my hero personally! He was a keen angler, and I used to go fishing with him. On these occasions I was able to observe him from an entirely different viewpoint and got to know the man, not merely the image. And the nearer I got, the smaller he became.
>
> But God eventually led that downcast schoolboy to a new hero. And I have walked with my Jesus for thirty-five years now. In that time I have often disappointed him, but he has never disappointed me! I have got to know him better, and the nearer I get, the bigger he becomes.[1]

Jesus is sufficient

Peter's illustration captures the heart of what this book is all about. God delights in blessing us. He has given us all things richly to enjoy: 'Every good and perfect gift is from above, coming down from the Father of the heavenly lights, who does not change like shifting shadows' (James 1:17).

Everything good in this world – families, music, sunny days, showers of rain, love and laughter, poetry and pineapples – comes from his hand. It would be churlish to despise any gift that our generous Father bestows on us. But the tendency of the human heart, as we saw earlier, is to cherish the gift and forget the Giver. The moment that our focus moves away from God, we begin to love and live for the wrong things, and they become idols. The result is inevitable disappointment, for nothing in this world is designed to give ultimate satisfaction. Except for one. The closer we get to Jesus, the bigger he becomes. He never disappoints. In this chapter we are going to spend a little time gazing at the glory of Christ. This is one sure antidote to the disappointment that comes when our affections are pulled elsewhere.

We could open the New Testament anywhere and we would find this message of the all-sufficiency of Jesus Christ.

Here's what Jesus himself claimed: 'The thief comes only to steal and kill and destroy; I have come that they may have life, and have it to the full' (John 10:10).

He is the bread of life who satisfies our souls; he is the light of the world who illuminates our darkness; he is the resurrection and the life, who walks with us through the valley of the shadow of death and brings us safely home (John 6:35, 48, 51; 8:12; 11:25). He is the good shepherd who meets all the needs of his flock (John 10:11, 14).

Think of the words of Peter when asked whether he would desert Jesus, like so many others had: 'Lord, to whom shall we go? You have the words of eternal life' (John 6:68).

Or think of the book of Hebrews.

Here we meet Jesus, the all-sufficient Saviour – greater than angels, or Moses or the whole Old Testament system of religion. We don't need anything other than him for a full and complete salvation:

> Therefore, brothers and sisters, since we have confidence to enter the Most Holy Place by the blood of Jesus, by a new and living way opened for us through the curtain, that is, his body, and since we have a great priest over the house of God, let us draw near to God with a sincere heart and with the full assurance that faith brings, having our hearts sprinkled to cleanse us from a guilty conscience and having our bodies washed with pure water. (Hebrews 10:19–22)

It is the master theme of the apostle Paul. He asserts, 'I can do all things through him [Christ] who strengthens me' (Philippians 4:13 NKJV).

And again,

> It is because of him that you are in Christ Jesus, who has become for us wisdom from God – that is, our righteousness, holiness and redemption. Therefore, as it is written: 'Let the one who boasts boast in the Lord.'
> (1 Corinthians 1:30–31)

More of Christ – not more than Christ

Let's see how Paul develops this important theme of Christ's sufficiency in the first chapter of his letter to the Colossians.

Paul is imprisoned in Rome when he hears from this church. The news from Colossae is incredibly encouraging:

> The gospel is bearing fruit and growing throughout the whole world – just as it has been doing among you since the day you heard it and truly understood God's grace. You learned it from Epaphras, our dear fellow servant, who is a faithful minister of Christ on our behalf, and who also told us of your love in the Spirit.
> (Colossians 1:6–8)

However, there is a serious problem. False teachers have arrived and are saying that the Colossian Christians need more than Jesus. He is a good place to begin, but you need to go beyond him and graduate to a greater knowledge and a higher spirituality. Jesus is the equivalent of a GCSE or perhaps an A level. But the teachers have more to offer: a postgraduate level of fuller knowledge and deeper wisdom.

When Paul hears this, he goes ballistic! How can they be so foolish! How can they abandon what they have? 'For in Him

dwells all the fullness of the Godhead bodily; and you are complete in Him, who is the head of all principality and power'
(Colossians 2:9–10 NKJV).

You are complete in Christ – why would you seek anything
else? Paul's response to the false teachers is very clear: 'You do
not need more than Christ; you need more of Christ.'

This is the theme he has picked up on in the first chapter:

> The Son is the image of the invisible God, the firstborn over
> all creation. For in him all things were created: things in heaven
> and on earth, visible and invisible, whether thrones or powers
> or rulers or authorities; all things have been created through
> him and for him. He is before all things, and in him all things
> hold together. And he is the head of the body, the church; he
> is the beginning and the firstborn from among the dead, that in
> everything he may have the supremacy. For God was pleased to
> have all his fullness dwell in him, and through him to reconcile
> to himself all things, whether things on earth or things in heaven,
> by making peace through his blood, shed on the cross.
> (Colossians 1:15–20)

As we consider this amazing statement together, remember that
we are doing this as an antidote to the desire to find ultimate
satisfaction in anything other than Jesus. As we gaze at his glory,
we will find ourselves nourished by his beauty and satisfied with
his sufficiency.

Jesus, the firstborn over creation

Paul begins with the 'cosmic Christ' as he reflects on the
relationship of Christ to the creation (Colossians 1:15–18). Jesus
is the 'image of the invisible God'. We've seen how the Bible
forbids the use of idols. Yet humans have a built-in predisposition
to worship the creation rather than the Creator. This is both an

affront to God's majesty and a foolish misdirection of faith. What could be more irrational than trusting a block of wood to meet your needs?

However, Jesus of Nazareth, the carpenter from Galilee, is the perfect and final revelation of God. He is not merely a pointer to God or the best illustration of deity, but an exact representation of the nature and character of God. In him the invisible becomes visible, the intangible becomes tangible and the eternal draws close. He is not a diluted form of God – he is deity at the highest possible setting.

As the one who is fully divine, he has a particular relationship with the cosmos – he is the 'firstborn over all creation'. This title is a reference to his position, rank, dignity and function. He holds the rights of the firstborn – the position of ultimate honour in a universe that depends on him for its very existence. The universe was created by him and for him, and he is the one who holds it together. He is its author and governor and goal. It exists with a view to his glory.

What a stunning statement!

So everything we see, feel, hear, touch or taste is under the lordship of Jesus Christ. The man from Nazareth is master of everything: oceans and deserts, mountains and forests, Niagara Falls and the Grand Canyon, blue whales and plankton, subatomic particles and star systems, the DNA double helix and spinning galaxies. He is also master of the invisible realm: the forces of evil headed by the devil and the angelic hosts who are swift to obey God's will, all must bow before his throne. He is the origin and destiny of every object we have ever seen, every person we have ever met and every thought we have ever entertained.

At the heart of the cosmos is a Person – someone we can know and trust and love. We do not live in a cold, mechanical universe abandoned by an absentee landlord. The sun rises because he wills it; our hearts beat because he ordains it; the world continues at his say-so. He is the cement and support of the cosmos. All of life's questions find their answer in him.

When we are tempted to seek ultimate satisfaction in anything other than Jesus, disappointment is inevitable. How could we be so foolish? Why seek anything more than Christ when you already have everything in Christ?

Jesus, the firstborn over the church

But there is more.

As this creation has been scarred by sin, the Creator has every right to walk away from it. But instead of washing his hands, as we saw earlier, he has rolled up his sleeves and entered the world he made to put it right.

The second half of this stupendous statement closely resembles the first. But here the emphasis is not on the original creation, but on the new creation, with its focus on the church (Colossians 1:18–20).

Jesus is the head of the church. It belongs to him by right. His sacrifice on the cross and his resurrection from the dead brought it into existence. He is 'the beginning and firstborn from among the dead'. The turning point in history was the moment when Jesus rose from the grave. This is the solid foundation on which the New Testament is based.

The resurrection of Jesus is *historical*. It is not a fable or a parable. It was a literal, physical and datable event in history. The body that was laid in the tomb was the same body that rose from the dead three days later. The apostles saw him, heard him and touched him. They watched him eat a piece of fish. They knew the difference between a ghost and a real man.

The resurrection of Jesus is *rational*. Faith is not 'believing something that isn't true', but confidence based on evidence. The evidence that Jesus rose has been debated and discussed and scrutinized for years. It continues to bear the weight that Christians attach to it.[2]

The resurrection of Jesus is *empirical*. In the resurrection all the plaintive cries of the human heart are answered. As human beings, we are hard-wired for eternity. Something inside us cries out for purpose and forgiveness, for love and hope, for a relationship with God. A risen Christ is the answer to the inbuilt longing of the human heart. Christianity is not true because it works; rather, it works because it is true.

Returning to Colossians, we learn that the one who has conquered death is none other than God himself. God 'was pleased to have all his fullness dwell in him'. Only God could bring about the purposes of God. And those purposes are cosmic. They are nothing less than the reconciliation of the universe with its Creator. The resurrection of Christ gives hope to the whole cosmos that the stain of sin can be removed for ever.

The resurrection of Jesus changes everything.

It is as if the *Titanic* could be turned from colliding with the iceberg just seconds before one of the most famous catastrophes in history. The cosmos is mutilated by the graffiti of sin and doomed to destruction. When Jesus rises from the dead, he turns everything around. Death is defeated, hope is reborn and the universe is redeemed. History does not end in the cul-de-sac of death. A rebellious universe will be brought back into submission to its Creator. Enmity will be removed. Harmony will be restored. Christ will reign for ever in a world dominated by the shalom of God.

How could we not be satisfied with this Christ? Just think of it: our Captain and our King, our Friend and our Master, our older Brother and our God.

'Through his blood, shed on the cross'

But there is one last phrase that is the capstone to Paul's reflections.

The resurrection does not stand alone as the determining event in human history. Jesus made peace 'through his blood, shed on the cross'. Paul is amazingly graphic here. He might have made an oblique reference to the death of Jesus. Instead, he is very clear that this took place when he shed his blood on a cross. After all the sublime descriptions of Jesus, the two words 'blood' and 'cross' are jarring. The one who is fully God is also a true man with real blood flowing through his veins. And he did not die in a quiet, dignified way. He was nailed to a cross and put on public display like a slab of meat hanging in an abattoir. Crucifixion was the ultimate deterrent in the Roman Empire. Death was deliberately slow, painful and public. It was also the height of shame and degradation.

For the Jews, it had an added repugnance. Anyone hung up in public was obviously under the curse of God (Deuteronomy 21:23). Stoning was too good for Jesus. Crucify him, and you have ended his Messianic pretensions for ever.

You would expect Paul to brush it under the carpet, but instead, he heralds it from the rooftops. The cost of redemption and a reconciled universe is the price that Jesus paid when he died in our place. He became the lightning rod for the wrath of God against our sins. The wrath is spent, and now God smiles on all who come to him through Jesus Christ:

> Christ redeemed us from the curse of the law by becoming a curse for us, for it is written: 'Cursed is everyone who is hung on a pole.' He redeemed us in order that the blessing given to Abraham might come to the Gentiles through Christ Jesus, so that by faith we might receive the promise of the Spirit.
> (Galatians 3:13–14)

Without the cross, 'the holiness of God would terrify us, his power would crush us, his justice would condemn us and his eternity would be our greatest nightmare'.[3] Because of the cross, his power is our protection, his holiness is our delight, his justice is our justification and his eternity is our glorious destiny.

The darling of heaven

I started my preaching in small village chapels in Wiltshire. Once a year I visited a small church and was always greeted by the secretary: 'Hello, my name is Mr Marsh. I'm the secretary. I'm so glad you have come. If the Lord spares me, on my next birthday I will be ninety-six years old.'

Every year I went to the church. It was always the same greeting – with a slight adjustment due to the passing of another birthday. So it continued, until the time came for a momentous announcement. Greeting me as usual, Mr Marsh proclaimed, 'Hello, my name is Mr Marsh. I'm the secretary. I'm so glad you have come. If the Lord spares me, next birthday I will be 100 years old, and then I have decided to retire as church secretary!'

I thought it was a little slack myself!

But that was not the most memorable thing about my visits to this little chapel. What impressed me most were his prayers. In a mellifluous Wiltshire accent, he would always pray,

> O Father, thank you so much for bringing this young man to us today. Now we plead with you, please show us Jesus. He is the darling of heaven and he is the darling of our hearts.

Mr Marsh was a farmer who spent all his life in a small Wiltshire village – just like his father and his grandfather before him. In a long life he must have experienced many disappointments. Longevity only adds to their quantity. But he had learned a secret that the preacher in the opening section of this chapter had learned. Jesus is 'the darling of heaven, and he is the darling of our hearts'. The closer we get to him, the bigger he becomes. He is the only one who will never disappoint us.

How much we all need to learn that lesson.

Questions

1. Consider these other great passages about Jesus:

   - John 1:1–18
   - Philippians 2:5–11
   - Hebrews 1:14

   How do they add to our understanding of the magnificence of our Saviour?

2. 'Where do we come from? What are we? Where are we going?' How does the cosmic Christ help us to answer these questions?

3. 'A risen Christ is the answer to the inbuilt longing of the human heart.' What are these longings? How does the risen Christ meet them?

4. Jesus warned the Christians in Ephesus about losing their first love (Revelation 2:4). Look at this passage. What causes us to drift away from Jesus? What is the way back?

5. How does knowing the fullness and sufficiency of Jesus help us when we are disappointed?

12. Gratitude attitudes: guard your heart

In the seventeenth century the Thirty Years War (1618–1648) ravaged Europe. It seemed as if the Four Horsemen of the Apocalypse had been released. The walled city of Eilenburg in Saxony was at the centre of the storm. The economy collapsed and it became overcrowded as refugees flocked into the town. Soon plague had invaded the streets.

It was 1673, known as 'the year of great pestilence'. There were four Christian pastors in the town. One of them abandoned his post, and two of them died. The one remaining, Martin Rinkart, a German Lutheran, conducted the funerals of his clerical brothers. Over the next few years he conducted a total of 4,480 funerals – as many as forty to fifty each day. He officiated at the funeral of his own wife.

Living under the shadow of death, Rinkart wrote a prayer for his children. It became a popular hymn, remarkable when you remember the circumstances of its composition:

Now thank we all our God,
with heart and hands and voices,
who wondrous things hath done,

in whom his world rejoices;
who from our mother's arms
hath blessed us on our way
with countless gifts of love,
and still is ours today.

O may this bounteous God
through all our life be near us,
with ever joyful hearts
and blessèd peace to cheer us;
and keep us in his grace,
and guide us when perplexed,
and free us from all ills
in this world and the next.

All praise and thanks to God
the Father now be given,
the Son, and him who reigns
with them in highest heaven,
the one eternal God,
whom earth and heaven adore;
for thus it was, is now,
and shall be evermore.[1]

What we can control

We cannot control the external circumstances of our lives.

This is the clear and demonstrative theme of the Bible. Think back to chapter 2. We live outside the Garden – between the curse-free world of Genesis 1 – 2 and the curse-freed world of Revelation 21 – 22.

Disappointment is inevitable, because we never quite achieve the things we aim for. The things we had hoped for either fail to materialize, or they fail to satisfy, or they fail to last. Whether they are legitimate and wholesome, or sinful and harmful, nothing short of God will ever satisfy. We know this, but we constantly forget it and find ourselves stranded on Disappointment Island yet again. What we expected just does not match what we actually find. Job speaks of those who trust in anything but God:

> What they trust in is fragile;
>> what they rely on is a spider's web.
> They lean on the web, but it gives way;
>> they cling to it, but it does not hold.
> (Job 8:14–15)

What a powerful picture of the insubstantiality of human dreams – a flimsy cobweb that will not bear the weight entrusted to it. Catch a glimpse of a sunbeam refracted through a raindrop on a cobweb, and it looks substantial and beautiful. But the wind blows and all is gone. Such is life with all its hopes and joys.

We cannot control the external circumstances of our lives. But we can control our reaction to them. With God's help, we can control our hearts.

The heart is the centre of our emotional-intellectual-moral activity. It is the heart and its desires that drive us as human beings. It is the entire inner life of a person:

> Above all else, guard the heart,
>> for everything you do flows from it.
> (Proverbs 4:23)

How our hearts respond to disappointment will make or break us. God calls us to demonstrate thankfulness and joy in all circumstances – whether those circumstances lead to elation or disappointment.

As good as dead

Human beings find it much easier to complain than to be thankful. Grumpiness and griping come more naturally than grace and gratitude.

The Bible is replete with examples of ingratitude. Israel forgot God's goodness to them and constantly complained of their circumstances (Exodus 17:1–3; Deuteronomy 32:18). David's sin with Bathsheba stemmed from failure to remember all God's mercies (2 Samuel 12:7–14). People instinctively know that they owe their lives to God, but they ignore him and seek to act without reference to him (Romans 1:21).

The way our hearts react to disappointments will determine the direction of our lives. If we allow grumbling and criticism to grip our hearts, then we will struggle with disappointment and allow it to shape our whole outlook. If, on the other hand, we cultivate grateful and thankful hearts, we will learn to deal with disappointments in a God-honouring way.

What does a grateful heart look like? Let's consider the example of an unnamed Samaritan outcast.

In Luke 17 Jesus is on the journey to Jerusalem and the cross. In Samaria he is hailed by ten lepers (Luke 17:11–19). These men had a 'dreaded skin disease' (Luke 17:12 GNT). This is no exaggeration. If you suspected that you were infected with leprosy, you went to see the priest. If leprosy was confirmed, you were immediately ostracized. You did not return home to say goodbye to your family. Never again would you kiss your wife or hug your children. You tore your clothes as a sign of mourning. Your family will hold a funeral. You are as good as dead.

Reduced to begging, your only company will be poor souls suffering with the same disease as you. Social and religious barriers disappear. Jews have no dealings with Samaritans. But here are Jews and Samaritans united in common adversity. If you are sleeping rough on an icy winter's night, you do not mind who shares your blanket. Any human contact is welcome.

Over the next few years you will watch as the disease ravages your body. You will lose the sensitivity in your fingers and toes. Your extremities will rot and be damaged beyond repair. You will be disfigured so badly that even your closest friend will no longer recognize you.

There is no way back. There is no hope. Lepers do not get better.

But then they hear about Jesus.

They approach him as he is about to enter the town. In a loud voice they cry for mercy. They receive far more from Jesus than they might have anticipated. He tells them to go and show themselves to the priest. This is what cured lepers did.

And on the way they are healed. Crooked limbs straighten. Gnarled fingers unbend. Eruptions in the skin are smoothed. For the first time in years feeling returns, and health surges through the body. It is almost impossible to imagine the amazement that these broken men suddenly feel.

Nine of the Jewish lepers continue on their way to the local priest. He is their access to normality. With a certificate of health in their hands, they can return to their previous existence. Relationships can be mended, careers resumed and life can start again – amazing.

Thankfulness

But one man recognizes that there is another priority, and he returns to thank Jesus. His thanksgiving is extravagant and profuse: 'One of them, when he saw he was healed, came back, praising God in a loud voice. He threw himself at Jesus' feet and thanked him – and he was a Samaritan' (Luke 17:15–16).

Amazingly, it is the Samaritan heretic who remembers Jesus.

Jesus is shocked at the ingratitude of the nine who did not return. He asks three questions which reveal his surprise:

'Were not all ten cleansed? Where are the other nine? Has no one returned to give praise to God except this foreigner?'

How is such ingratitude possible?

'Rise and go; your faith has made you well' (Luke 17:19) might be translated: 'Your faith has brought you salvation.' This man has received more than physical healing – he has come into a relationship with God through Jesus. His physical healing is symbolic of the fuller and more magnificent gift of eternal life.

Are you still amazed?

And here is the heart and thrust of the story. If we are Christians, we should be amazed at the grace of God that has rescued us from hell and given us the assurance of heaven. It is hard to imagine the depth of pain and alienation experienced by the leper in the story – that is why I have described it in graphic terms. But we all know the depth of spiritual pain and eternal alienation which God has rescued us from. Only a failure to remember this will breed ingratitude.

A Christian is a man or a woman who has never ceased to be amazed that God could save them. Like Charles Wesley, we are open-mouthed with wonder:

And can it be that I should gain
An interest in the Saviour's blood?
Died He for me, who caused His pain –
For me, who Him to death pursued?
Amazing love! How can it be,
That Thou, my God, shouldst die for me?

And in a less-familiar verse in this great hymn Wesley confesses,

Still the small inward voice I hear,
That whispers all my sins forgiven;

Still the atoning blood is near,
That quenched the wrath of hostile Heaven.
I feel the life His wounds impart;
I feel the Saviour in my heart.[2]

Do we feel this? Are we still amazed? Does the magnitude of God's grace leave us lost in wonder and praise?

Gratitude is a choice

In his classic book on the parable of the prodigal son, Henri Nouwen writes,

> The discipline of gratitude is the explicit effort to acknowledge that all I am and have is given to me as a gift of love, a gift to be celebrated with joy.
>
> Gratitude as a discipline involves a conscious choice. I can choose to be grateful even when my emotions and feelings are still steeped in hurt and resentment. It is amazing how many occasions present themselves in which I can choose gratitude instead of complaint. I can choose to be grateful when I am criticized, even when my heart still responds in bitterness. I can choose to speak about goodness and beauty, even when my inner eye still looks for someone to accuse or something to call ugly. I can choose to listen to the voices that forgive and to look at the faces that smile, even while I still hear words of revenge and see grimaces of hatred.
>
> There is always the choice between resentment and gratitude because God has appeared in my darkness, urged me to come home, and declared in a voice filled with affection: 'You are with me always, and all I have is yours.'
>
> The choice for gratitude rarely comes without some real effort. But each time I make it, the next choice is a little easier, a little freer, a little less self-conscious.[3]

So gratitude is a choice. No matter how dire our circumstances may be, the gospel always gives us ample reasons to be grateful. And a grateful heart will lead to thankful lips.

Listen to the advice of Andrew Murray:

> Let us thank God heartily as often as we pray that we have His Spirit in us to teach us to pray. Thanksgiving will draw our hearts out to God and keep us engaged with Him; it will take our attention from ourselves and give the Spirit room in our hearts.[4]

A grateful heart and thankful lips are two of the great antidotes to disappointment.

The citadel of the mind is ours to command. We must choose what we think about. Paul gives clear instructions about this:

> Finally, brothers and sisters, whatever is true, whatever is noble, whatever is right, whatever is pure, whatever is lovely, whatever is admirable – if anything is excellent or praiseworthy – think about such things.
> (Philippians 4:8)

The unnamed Samaritan would have strongly approved of the second stanza of Rinkart's great hymn:

> O may this bounteous God
> through all our life be near us,
> with ever-joyful hearts
> and blessèd peace to cheer us;
> and keep us in his grace,
> and guide us when perplexed,
> and free us from all ills
> in this world and the next.

Questions

1. Read Rinkart's hymn. What are the causes for thanksgiving that he identifies?
2. What does the Bible mean by 'the heart'?
3. What are the results of ingratitude? How can we cultivate a thankful heart?
4. Read through Paul's short letter to the Philippians and make a note of all the references to:

   - Christ
   - Joy and thankfulness

   What can we learn when we put these references side by side?
5. John Piper defines Christian joy in this way:

   > Christian joy is a good feeling in the soul, produced by the Holy Spirit, as he causes us to see the beauty of Christ in the word and in the world.[5]

   How does this help us to understand the nature of joy?
6. How does a thankful and joyful heart sustain us through disappointment? Are you investing wisely in this area?

Home at last

13. Giving what we love most

The city of Cambridge is famous for its magnificent historical churches and chapels. The People's Mission was not one of them. It was in this small and ramshackle tin tabernacle that I preached my first sermon on a cold February day in 1974.

The congregation was meagre and elderly. It had survived with the support of young undergraduates from the university who cut their homiletical teeth there. I had spoken to groups of young people before, but never to a whole church. I asked advice from a pastor friend, and he said, 'Preach on a passage that has meant something to you.' So I chose Genesis 22.

This chapter is one of the most poignant and moving passages in the whole Bible. God tells Abraham to take the most precious thing he has – his beloved son, Isaac – and sacrifice him as a burnt offering on Mount Moriah. The story resonates with many truths, but it seemed to me then that there was one overwhelming question that God was asking of Abraham: 'Do you love me enough to give me the most precious thing you have?'

At the time I was praying for my mum and dad to come to faith. If you had pushed me, I think I would have said that nothing was more important to me than that. The Sunday before I was due to preach, my dad had come to visit me. He was, as you will remember, a working-class bloke and he had made huge sacrifices to enable me to study in Cambridge. I was proud of him and loved him to bits. I had the opportunity to share my faith with him before he left on the coach. I went to my room and began to think about the sermon for the following week. It was at that point that I decided to preach from Genesis 22 and to emphasize the cost of discipleship.

I loved my dad and mum – but did I love them more than I loved God?

Father Abraham

The story of Abraham is found in the early chapters of Genesis (chapters 12 – 25). He is a key figure in the developing purpose of God. The world has rebelled against God by trying to build a tower that will reach to heaven (Genesis 11), but God confuses their languages and scatters them. He then calls one man to follow him and be the channel through whom he will bless all nations.

The story begins with the call to leave everything that he knows and go where God directs him. He dwells in the Fertile Crescent, first in Ur and then in Haran. Ur was a magnificent city with libraries and parks, large three-storey houses with central heating and massive ziggurats. God tells him to leave all this behind – all that is safe and familiar – and to follow him into an unknown future (Genesis 12:1). Obedience will lead to blessing: a name, a place and a people (12:2–3, 7). Abraham obeys and goes (12:4).

The rest of the story charts the downs and ups of Abraham's experience: the errors of judgment and moments of downright disobedience, the maturing faith and the constant experience of God's faithfulness. And all the time Abraham is waiting for the one thing that can confirm God's promises and be the channel through which blessing will come to the nations: the gift of a son. From a New Testament perspective, we know that the birth of this son is a vital link in the chain that will one day result in the birth of Jesus, through whom the blessing of God will spill over into the nations. The promises to Abraham will be realized in all who believe in Jesus:

> Christ redeemed us from the curse of the law by becoming a curse for us, for it is written: 'Cursed is everyone who is hung on a pole.' He redeemed us in order that the blessing given to Abraham might come to the Gentiles through Christ Jesus, so that by faith we might receive the promise of the Spirit.
> (Galatians 3:13–14)

But God keeps him waiting.

After twenty-five years Abraham is as good as dead as far as having children is concerned. Only then does God act in a miraculous way, and Sarah becomes pregnant.

Genesis 21 feels like the climax of the story:

> Now the LORD was gracious to Sarah as he had said, and the LORD did for Sarah what he had promised. Sarah became pregnant and bore a son to Abraham in his old age, at the very time God had promised him. Abraham gave the name Isaac to the son Sarah bore him.
> (Genesis 21:1–3)

The name Isaac means 'he laughs', referring to the initial response of Sarah to the news of the birth (Genesis 18:12–15). God filled their house with laughter and their lives with joy. Abraham settled down for some time in the beautiful city of Beersheba (21:32–34).

One expects to read, '. . . and they all lived happily ever after'.

The test God designed

And then we come to Genesis 22.

There is a time gap between these two chapters, at least long enough for Isaac to grow up and be sufficiently old to accompany his father on the mission to Moriah. God summons Abraham as he has done many times before. On previous occasions God has spoken words of encouragement and hope. But this time his words are like a stab in the heart: 'Take your son, your only son, whom you love – Isaac – and go to the region of Moriah. Sacrifice him there as a burnt offering on a mountain that I will show you' (22:2).

Are these the cruellest words in the Bible?

Abraham is a wealthy man, but God does not ask for his flocks or his treasures. God demands his son. And he is specific: it is his only son, Isaac. Abraham did have another son, but Isaac is the son through whom all the promises of God are going to be realized. Coming after all those years of waiting, it is not surprising that he is described as the son whom Abraham loves. If you have children, you will understand. We take our kids in our arms and ache with love for them. We would do anything to protect them. But Abraham is not to protect him; he is to kill him. The command is clear and unambiguous. Travel for three days to Moriah and there bind your son, lay him on an altar, kill him and burn his body so that nothing is left.

There is no wriggle room, no possibility of misunderstanding. Abraham is to do this with his own hands. There is to be a holocaust, and the thing he loves most in the world is to go up in smoke.

This was a test at so many levels.

At the most basic level, it is the test of a parent's heart. Do I trust God with my children? Can I give him the lives of those who are dearest to me?

It is also a test of understanding. Isaac is the channel through whom God's promises and purposes are to be realized. What God will do *through* Isaac is a direct contradiction to what God now tells Abraham to do *to* Isaac. The words in Genesis 22:2 are remarkably like those in the original call of Genesis 12:1. In each case there is a call to a specific threefold sacrifice: 'Go from your country, your people and your father's household', and 'take your son, your only son, whom you love'. But there is a massive difference. In Genesis 12 Abraham is being asked to give up his past and is assured of God's blessings for the future (12:2–3). In Genesis 22 he is being commanded to give up his future: all his hopes and dreams and expectations. And there is no accompanying promise.

At the most painful level of all, this is a test of his experience of God. What kind of God would ask such a thing? It was a common practice among the Canaanite tribes – their god Moloch demanded human sacrifice. Is Yahweh no better than this? Is he capricious? Can his promises be trusted? Is all that Abraham has ever believed about God just a creation of his own mind? Abraham is the only man in the Bible called the 'friend of God' (James 2:23) – is this any way to treat your friends?

And God still tests

Notice that the passage is very clear. God really tested Abraham. This was not a figment of his imagination, the fanatical dream of a disturbed mind. God's purpose will become clearer later in the passage, but at the beginning Abraham is forced to trust God in the dark – he does not know how things will work out.

And very often the disappointments of life are sent by God to test the depth of our love and the sincerity of our faith. Love makes us vulnerable. Abraham was right to love his son, but it is that 'rightness' which causes the pain.

I think of the couple who were so proud when their son followed God's call to serve him in cross-cultural mission. Then the news came that he was very sick due to complications following an infection. We prayed, but he died, away from the embrace of his parents on the other side of the world: 'If God loved us so much, why did he take our son? How could he be so cruel?' they wailed.

I remember the brokenness of the woman whose husband suddenly returned from a month of Christian ministry to tell her that he no longer loved her and there was someone else: 'I have made so many sacrifices to serve the Lord – why would he let my husband do this?' she cried.

When God tests – and he does – it is right for us to feel the pain of disappointment, but it is also vital that we understand the purpose of the test. The devil tempts us in order to destroy us. God tests us to establish us. God is incapable of tempting us to do wrong (James 1:13–18).

I used to teach religious education, as you will remember. The GCSE course in those days involved thirty multiple-choice questions on Luke's Gospel. One morning I found myself invigilating as my own students sat the paper. Jackie was the brightest of the group, and I expected her to ace the exam. I looked over her shoulder and, to my horror, saw that she had all the questions right, but a slight error at the beginning meant that they were slightly out of order. She would get no marks. Of course, I could not say anything, but kept passing her desk willing her to check the paper. With five minutes to go, she suddenly saw her error and asked for another computer printout to resubmit her answers.

She passed with flying colours.

When he tests us, God stands looking over our shoulder willing us to pass. The test may be painful – but his intentions are always beneficent.

Abraham's trust

Genesis 22:3 is remarkable:

Early the next morning Abraham got up and loaded his donkey. He took with him two of his servants and his son Isaac. When

he had cut enough wood for the burnt offering, he set out for
the place God had told him about.

His obedience is prompt. He does not try to steal more time with
Isaac, but he leaves early in the morning while the shepherds are
waking and the dew is still on the ground. Delayed obedience is
disobedience.

They travel for three days to reach Moriah. Can you imagine
the conversation? Can you picture the nights as Abraham stands
under the stars looking at his son as he gently sleeps? What
questions passed though Isaac's mind? What doubts gripped
Abraham's imagination?

Finally, they arrive at their destination, and Abraham and the
boy begin the weary climb up the mountain alone (22:4–8). Once
there, the narrative moves forward at fever pitch – notice the
sixfold use of the word 'and':

> Then they came to the place of which God had told him. *And*
> Abraham built an altar there *and* placed the wood in order; *and* he
> bound Isaac his son *and* laid him on the altar, upon the wood. *And*
> Abraham stretched out his hand *and* took the knife to slay his son.
> (22:9–10 NKJV, italics mine)

Abraham was ready to go ahead with it. He held nothing back.
Does Paul, in the New Testament, have this passage in mind
when he urges Christians, '. . . in view of God's mercy, to offer
your bodies as a living sacrifice, holy and pleasing to God – this
is your true and proper worship' (Romans 12:1)?

Christianity is more than a hobby – I am called to love God
with all my being, so that other loves pale by comparison (Luke
14:26). Am I willing to lay my time and my talents and my
treasures at the feet of Jesus?

But most of all, this is an obedience motivated by faith. It is
not the act of a fanatic, but the reasoned response of a man who
knows God. Abraham was convinced that even if Isaac died, God

would raise him from the dead. There are hints of this in Genesis 22:5: 'He said to his servants, "Stay here with the donkey while I and the boy go over there. We will worship and then we will come back to you."'

It is spelled out in the New Testament: 'Abraham reasoned that God could even raise the dead, and so in a manner of speaking he did receive Isaac back from death' (Hebrews 11:19).

Notice that faith is not opposed to reason – it begins with reason, but goes beyond it. Abraham recalled all he knew about God: God is wise and gracious and consistent; he cannot lie; he will not mislead. He remembered that the promises were to be fulfilled through Isaac. He put the two together and concluded that God would raise Isaac from the dead. He could trust God with the thing he loved most. Faith is not the last resort of the irrational. It is the first principle of any relationship. Trust is the glue that holds relationships together, without which they crash and burn.

Faith is risky, but it is inspired by confidence in the unchanging character of God. He calls us to trust him in the dark, based on what we have learned in the light. God is gentle, kind and patient. He is not an ogre who gives us good gifts only to hurt us by then taking them away. Past grace gives us confidence to trust God for future grace.

Disappointments – no matter how heart-rending – are designed to test and deepen our trust. Faith can reach maturity only by being stretched.

Mission accomplished – mission anticipated

At the last minute God stays Abraham's hand:

> 'Do not lay a hand on the boy,' he said. 'Do not do anything to him. Now I know that you fear God, because you have not withheld from me your son, your only son.'

> Abraham looked up and there in a thicket he saw a ram caught
> by its horns. He went over and took the ram and sacrificed it as
> a burnt offering instead of his son. So Abraham called that place
> The LORD Will Provide. And to this day it is said, 'On the
> mountain of the LORD it will be provided.'
> (22:12–14)

Abraham's faith is genuine, his love is sincere and his reverence
is real. He has passed the test, and God confirms his promises
with an oath (Genesis 22:15–18; Hebrews 6:13–14):

> I will surely bless you and make your descendants as numerous
> as the stars in the sky and as the sand on the seashore. Your
> descendants will take possession of the cities of their enemies,
> and through your offspring all nations on earth will be blessed,
> because you have obeyed me.
> (22:17–18)

Abraham returns with his son, knowing that God will bless the
whole world through his offspring.

Two thousand years later Jesus is born.

And Christians have long seen echoes of the life of Jesus in the
events of Genesis 22. Moriah is the place where Solomon built
the temple and it is the site of the crucifixion of Jesus, on that
green hill outside a city wall. As you see Isaac labouring up the
hill with a load on his back, can we not picture the shadow of
the Saviour? On the hilltop there are the Father and Son alone
together. Calvary is a noisy place until noon, when darkness
descends and the Father and Son are alone together as the eternal
salvation of lost people is transacted at terrible cost. The Son – the
young prince of glory – submits to the Father's will. The Father,
who has loved his Son with an everlasting and unclouded love, lays
the punishment for our sins on his Son and then turns his face away.

But unlike the Genesis story, there is no substitute. Or rather,
the Son himself is the substitute who takes our place and bears

our just punishment (Isaiah 53:4–6; 1 Peter 2:23–25). This time there is a real death and, of course, a real resurrection. God vindicates the Son who has obeyed his will and borne the punishment that we deserved.

> Here is love, vast as the ocean,
> loving kindness as the flood,
> when the Prince of life, our ransom,
> shed for us his precious blood.
> Who his love will not remember?
> Who can cease to sing his praise?
> He can never be forgotten
> throughout heaven's eternal days.
>
> On the mount of crucifixion
> fountains opened deep and wide;
> through the floodgates of God's mercy
> flowed a vast and gracious tide.
> Grace and love, like mighty rivers,
> poured incessant from above,
> and heaven's peace and perfect justice
> kissed a guilty world in love.[1]

Can I trust God?

We return to the key question which disappointment raises. When I cannot trace God's hand, can I trust his heart? I don't need to understand everything – I just want to be sure that he is worth it.

And our answer is Calvary. Here is love on display as never before. 'Here is love, vast as the ocean.' Paul is clear:

> What, then, shall we say in response to these things? If God is
> for us, who can be against us? He who did not spare his own Son,

but gave him up for us all – how will he not also, along with him, graciously give us all things?

(Romans 8:31–32)

Remember the bereaved couple who asked the question: 'If God loved us so much, why did he take our son? How could he be so cruel?' They will carry their pain for the rest of their lives, and there will be moments when it will seem unbearable. But the wife was also able to confide, 'In our bleakest moments we remember that God knows. After all, he gave his own Son for our sake.'

God is not an infinite iceberg – he is the Father of our Lord Jesus Christ who freely surrendered his Son so that we might be reconciled to him. This is the ultimate love story in the universe:

> To some, the image of a pale body glimmering on a dark night whispers of defeat. What good is a God who does not control his Son's suffering? But another sound can be heard: the shout of a God crying out to human beings, 'I LOVE YOU.' Love was compressed for all history in that lonely figure on the cross, who said that he could call down angels at any moment on a rescue mission, but chose not to – because of us. At Calvary, God accepted his own unbreakable terms of justice. Any discussion of how pain and suffering fit into God's scheme ultimately leads back to the cross.[2]

Can we trust God? Look at the cross.

Remember that little tin tabernacle in Cambridge? During the week after my father visited, I prepared my first sermon. As I did so, I continued to pray for my parents.

On the Wednesday morning there was a letter from my dad:

> On the way back I read that little book you gave me. When I got home, I got down by my bed and asked Jesus to be my Saviour. Is that OK?

You bet!

Can we trust him with the things we love most? Absolutely!

Questions

1. Read James 1:2–17. How can we distinguish the tests of God from the temptations of the devil?
2. What lessons did Abraham learn though his test?
3. Read the first two chapters of Job:

   - What did Job lose?
   - Why did he lose it?
   - How did he respond?

4. Reread Genesis 22. What are the similarities and differences between this story and the accounts of the crucifixion?

14. The power of hope

I met Tadeusz on my first visit to Poland.

After a short flight, the plane landed at the airport of Bydgoszcz. As I waited for my luggage, I rehearsed in my mind what I was supposed to do. I was due to speak in the ancient city of Toruń, birthplace of the astronomer Nicolaus Copernicus. A Polish pastor, identified as Tadeusz, would meet me at Arrivals and take me to the city, which was about 31 miles (about 50 km) away. I turned over in my mind the series of talks I had agreed to give, and then suddenly it struck me: I did not know Tadeusz. I could not recognize him and I didn't know a word of Polish. What if he wasn't there?

With some trepidation, I picked up my bags and followed the crowds to Arrivals. A couple of flights must have arrived together, so the place was heaving with people. But one individual stood out. Right at the front there was a giant of a man. He was dressed in a grey pinstripe suit and the loudest Hawaiian shirt you have ever seen. The ensemble was completed with bare feet and open-toed sandals – and all this in the middle of a Polish winter.

As I approached the concourse, I breathed what I thought was a perfectly reasonable prayer: 'Please, Lord, guide me to Tadeusz – but please let him not be the man in the sandals.'

But of course, he was!

He seemed to recognize me immediately. 'Pastor Mallard, welcome to my country,' he said warmly, as he enveloped me in a crushing bear-hug. He picked up my bags – I think he could have picked me up too if he had wanted to – and led me to his car. For such a big man, he had a very small car. He shoehorned himself into the driver's side, and we began a memorable journey. You are supposed to drive on the right-hand side of the road in Poland, but it was as if no-one had told Tadeusz that. We seemed to swerve wherever the mood took him. This was compounded by the fact that he had the disconcerting habit of wanting to look me in the eye whenever he addressed me. So I prayed as never before!

Eventually, we arrived and we had a great week of meetings. I got to love Tadeusz as a brother and respect him as a pastor.

At the end of the week he was due to take me back to the airport. I must confess that I was a little anxious, especially when he seemed to leave a very short time frame in which to make the journey. I think he must have picked up on my anxiety, because he reproved me:

> Pastor Paul, where is your faith? We are in Father's hands!
> Maybe it is Father's plan that you miss your flight, because this plane will crash and you will be saved. Or maybe you will miss it and the plane tomorrow will crash, and Father will take you home. Whatever happens, Father knows best.

A lifelong marathon

I caught my flight and am still here to tell the tale. But on the way home I reflected on Tadeusz's rough-and-ready theology. We are all in Father's hands. He is a Father whose plans are always in our best interest. We must get our disappointments in perspective. Glib and easy answers are of little use, but trusting

God's heart, even when we cannot see his hand, helps us to persevere.

And this is what this chapter is about.

We have journeyed a long way through the Land of Disappointment, but we are almost home. The disappointments of this life are acute and relentless, but the Father who loves us is preparing us for eternal joys for ever. We have one short life in which to experience disappointments. Father has eternity to make us happy in himself.

The New Testament is dominated by this 'living hope'. We could turn to a dozen passages to discover it, but come with me to Hebrews 12.

We do not know who wrote this great epistle, but its purpose seems clear. The author is writing to Messianic Jews, Jewish converts who have come to accept Jesus of Nazareth as their Messiah. They have experienced harassment in the past and stood firm, but now the persecution is getting worse. They are in danger of becoming discouraged and demoralized. They are being tempted to give up. The author writes a 'word of exhortation' (13:22), in which he argues that it might be difficult to go on, but it is impossible to go back.

To encourage them, he has two tactics.

First, he argues for the absolute supremacy and finality of Jesus Christ. He is the fulfilment of all the hopes and expectations of the Old Testament. He is God's last word – the Word incarnate in human flesh who is the radiance of God's glory. He is seated at God's right hand – the appointed heir of all things. To reject him is to reject God.

Second, he gives some of the most severe warnings in the Bible about the danger of desertion. If you reject Jesus, you have nowhere else to go. Those who continue to reject him have nothing to look forward to but judgment. It is a fearful thing to fall into the hands of the living God (Hebrews 10:31).

Towards the end of the letter he encourages them to persevere and keep their eyes on the goal:

> Therefore, since we are surrounded by such a great cloud
> of witnesses, let us throw off everything that hinders and the
> sin that so easily entangles. And let us run with perseverance the
> race marked out for us, fixing our eyes on Jesus, the pioneer and
> perfecter of faith. For the joy that was set before him he endured
> the cross, scorning its shame, and sat down at the right hand
> of the throne of God. Consider him who endured such opposition
> from sinners, so that you will not grow weary and lose heart.
> (Hebrews 12:1–3)

The race will be hard work: he uses a Greek word from which we get the word 'agony'. This is not a sprint or a jog in the park. It is more like a lifelong marathon across an obstacle course. Jesus promised his disciples that they would be completely fearless, absurdly happy and always in trouble.

As they must run with diligence, two things drive them on: a promise of encouragement and a word of instruction.

A promise of encouragement
The promise of encouragement is a reminder that we are not alone.

We are surrounded by 'a great cloud of witnesses' (12:1). The author is clearly referring to the examples of faith outlined in Hebrews 11. Here we have a long list of men and women who faced numerous obstacles in life, but persevered and did not give up. It is easy to commend these people as heroes of the faith, but we should remember that they were all flawed human beings. Noah (as we saw earlier) got drunk; Abraham lied about his wife and endangered her; Jacob was a cheat and a scoundrel; Moses was a convicted murderer. They often stumbled as we do, and yet they are commended. Why? Because they trusted God. This is what marked them out. They kept their eye on the goal and persevered, even when the wind of adversity blew in their faces. They kept going, even though in this life they did not receive all that God had promised:

These were all commended for their faith, yet none of them
received what had been promised, since God had planned
something better for us so that only together with us would
they be made perfect.

(11:39–40)

And in case we imagine that their faith protected them from
trials, he reminds us,

There were others who were tortured, refusing to be released
so that they might gain an even better resurrection. Some faced
jeers and flogging, and even chains and imprisonment. They were
put to death by stoning; they were sawn in two; they were killed
by the sword. They went about in sheepskins and goatskins,
destitute, persecuted and ill-treated – the world was not worthy
of them. They wandered in deserts and mountains, living in caves
and in holes in the ground.

(11:35–38)

Be encouraged by their example, says our author. You have the
same God – you can trust him for the future.

We do not have to run this race alone.

In Bath, where I live, we have a half-marathon every year. I
love to watch the runners – for many, this is their one annual
attempt at anything approaching physical exertion. A couple of
years ago I stood next to two very noisy teenage girls who were
cheering every runner who passed. I was amazed at the breadth
of their knowledge – they seemed to know the names of half
the competitors. They called on them by name, and many
runners seemed to be reinvigorated by this personal encouragement. Then it dawned on me. They did not know the runners
personally at all; they were just reading the names on their vests.

We run in the track marks of Abraham and Moses and David,
of Peter and Paul and John, and of all the saints who followed.
What is more, we run in the fellowship of the church where

everyone knows your name and is there to cheer you on (Hebrews 10:23–35).

A word of instruction

What about the word of instruction?

The author reminds us that if we are to run successfully, we must throw off everything that slows us down. No athlete runs in a pair of heavy boots or an overcoat. Runners strip down to a decent minimum. In the same way, we need to cast off everything that gets in the way.

Some things will be obvious – the sins that cling so closely. We must wrestle with lust and greed and pride and bitterness, which threaten to invade our souls and hinder us in the race.

But other things are less obvious. Legitimate leisure activities, hobbies or personal passions can begin to hamper us. A good thing becomes a God thing – an idol of the heart. If, for some reason, God takes it away, we are deeply disappointed and find ourselves angry with him. As we have seen, we must learn that some good things can become 'tangled bine-stems'[1] that twist around our legs and trip us up. We need to guard our hearts from anything that threatens to take God's place.

Instead, we are to run the race with perseverance. When our legs feel like lead and our lungs are bursting, we must keep going. Run through the pain. Run when you feel as if you are about to hit the wall. Never give up. We need to follow the example of Paul, who could look back over a life of trials and challenges and still say,

> For I am already being poured out like a drink offering, and the time for my departure is near. I have fought the good fight, I have finished the race, I have kept the faith. Now there is in store for me the crown of righteousness, which the Lord, the righteous Judge, will award to me on that day – and not only to me, but also to all who have longed for his appearing.
> (2 Timothy 4:6–8)

Run with confidence

It may be hard work, but we can be confident about the future, and this confidence will propel us forward. Such confidence comes from a steady gaze at Jesus. We must consciously turn our thoughts towards him. If, like Peter, we gaze at the waves, we are sure to sink. Instead, we must concentrate all our attention on Jesus. It is easy to become absorbed with our feelings or weaknesses or circumstances. Instead, we are to let our minds be absorbed with him.

Jesus is the object of our faith. He pioneered our faith in the first place – he is the one who inspired faith in us when we first believed. And he is the one who will bring that faith to completion, perfecting it. Unlike the pacemaker who drops out of the race before the end, Jesus is the one who leads us all the way home. The Bible is full of assurances to help us when disappointment threatens to turn into despair:

> To him who is able to keep you from stumbling and to present
> you before his glorious presence without fault and with great
> joy – to the only God our Saviour be glory, majesty, power and
> authority, through Jesus Christ our Lord, before all ages, now
> and for evermore! Amen.
> (Jude 24–25)

And Jesus is also the supreme example of persevering faith. Consider what he endured for us, remembering what you read earlier. He surrendered the glory of heaven for the shame of Golgotha. Instead of the song of angels, his ears were filled with the scorn of soldiers. He exchanged joys at the Father's right hand for the sting of nails and the stab of a spear. We must not minimize the horror with which Jesus approached the cross. He knew that he would face a brutal, vile and vicious death.

But there was more. On the cross he would face a unique and unprecedented experience. The Son who enjoyed an eternal and unclouded relationship with the Father would, for the first time, enter the darkness of condemnation when God placed the guilt of our sins on him and then punished him as if he were responsible for them all.

Charles Spurgeon expresses it vividly:

> The heart of Christ became like a reservoir in the midst
> of the mountains. All the tributary streams of iniquity, and
> every drop of the sins of his people, ran down and gathered
> into one vast lake, deep as hell and shoreless as eternity.
> All these met, as it were, in Christ's heart, and he endured
> them all.[2]

How did Jesus survive the horrors of what lay ahead of him? Our author tells us, 'For the joy that was set before him he endured the cross, scorning its shame, and sat down at the right hand of the throne of God' (12:2).

Jesus fixed his eyes on the joys of heaven that he would experience when he ascended to the Father's right hand. Like the athlete who sacrifices comfort and luxury for the anticipation of the medal or prize, so Jesus endured anguish and condemnation for the prize of heaven:

> After he has suffered,
>   he will see the light of life and be satisfied,
> by his knowledge my righteous servant will
>   justify many,
>   and he will bear their iniquities.
> Therefore I will give him a portion among the great,
>   and he will divide the spoils with the strong,
> because he poured out his life unto death,
>   and was numbered with the transgressors.
> For he bore the sin of many,
>   and made intercession for the transgressors.
> (Isaiah 53:11–12)

Christ has conquered death, and this conquest has implications for the whole cosmos.

Perhaps no-one has said this more eloquently than C. S. Lewis:

> The New Testament writers speak as if Christ's achievement in rising from the dead was the first event of its kind in the whole history of the universe. He is the 'first fruits', the 'pioneer of life'. He has forced open a door that has been locked since the death of the first man. He has met, fought, and beaten the King of Death. Everything is different because He has done so. This is the beginning of the New Creation: a new chapter in cosmic history has been opened.[3]

The rewards promised by the Father are universal and eternal in their dimensions.

We are called to follow Christ's example. The disappointments of this world are designed to make us homesick for heaven. We know that there is more. We long for a place where disappointment ceases to exist. Heaven will be a 'disappointment-free zone'.

Spring after winter

Heaven is often portrayed as the place where all the negative experiences of a broken world are gone for ever.

Think of the climax of Tolkien's *The Lord of the Rings*. Evil has finally been defeated:

> But Sam lay back, and stared with open mouth, and
> for a moment, between bewilderment and great joy,
> he could not answer. At last he gasped: 'Gandalf! I thought
> you were dead! But then I thought I was dead myself.
> Is everything sad going to come untrue? What's happened
> to the world?'

'A great Shadow has departed,' said Gandalf, and then he
laughed and the sound was like music, or water in a parched
land . . .

'How do I feel?' he cried. 'Well I don't know how to say it.
I feel, I feel' – he waved his arms in the air – 'I feel like spring
after winter, and sun on the leaves; and like trumpets and harps
and all the songs I have ever heard!'[4]

A great shadow has departed, and all pain is gone for ever. There
is no curse in that place of pure delight.

But this is only the negative hope of people familiar with pain.
The greatest blessing is the joy we can find in God alone.
Disappointments are messages from God designed to make us
homesick for heaven. We long for satisfaction, but nothing short
of God can ever satisfy us. Heaven will be the place of ultimate
satisfaction – its culmination. It is the exact reverse of our experience here. We've seen that disappointments arise because our
experience always falls short of our expectations. In heaven
our expectations will fall far short of our experience. Nothing in
heaven will disappoint; there will be no frustration or disillusionment; none of our desires will be thwarted. All that we
desired and hoped for will prove to be a pale picture of reality.

Imagine the expectations of the Pilgrim Fathers when they
landed at Plymouth Rock in 1620. Before them lay a glorious
new world, but all they knew was a short strip of land nestled
next to the Atlantic Ocean. Eking out a precarious existence for
the next few years, they were unaware of the nearly limitless
resources of the continent that lay before them. They knew
nothing of the Great Plains or the magnificence of the Rocky
Mountains; they were strangers to the mighty Mississippi and
Niagara Falls; they had never gazed on the deserts or forests or
lakes or canyons. They did not know that 3,000 miles west was
another immense ocean. And then there were the translucent
glaciers of the north and a thousand glittering islands in the
south.

Our experience of God now amounts to a brief sojourn on that thin slip of land we call life. We have the whole of eternity to taste that the Lord is good. Like explorers of a new world, we will see more and more and be for ever delighted by the magnificence of the God we adore. This passionate and joyful adoration of God is not merely an intellectual apprehension – it is the purpose of our existence. We are homesick for heaven. Only there will we come into the complete experience of the full divine beauty.

Listen to C. S. Lewis:

> If there lurks in most modern minds the notion that to desire our own good and earnestly to hope for the enjoyment of it is a bad thing, I submit that this notion has crept in from Kant and the Stoics and is no part of the Christian faith. Indeed, if we consider the unblushing promises of reward and the staggering nature of the rewards promised in the Gospels, it would seem that Our Lord finds our desires not too strong, but too weak. We are half-hearted creatures, fooling about with drink and sex and ambition when infinite joy is offered to us, like an ignorant child who wants to go on making mud pies in a slum because he cannot imagine what is meant by the offer of a holiday at the sea. We are far too easily pleased.[5]

And the occupation of heaven is the worship of this God. This delight will heal every disappointment we may ever have tasted in this life.

That moment

On 7 August 1954 England's Roger Bannister and Australia's John Landy met during the British Empire and Commonwealth Games in Vancouver. Both men had broken the four-minute barrier earlier that year. Their meeting was advertised as the ultimate showdown: the 'Miracle Mile'.

Landy led most of the way and thought that he had broken Bannister. But with ninety yards to go, Landy glanced over his left shoulder to check his opponent's position. Seizing his opportunity, Bannister shot past him and won the race. He would later describe this moment: 'I flung myself past Landy. As I did so I saw him glance over his opposite shoulder. This tiny act of his held great significance to me and gave me confidence.'[6]

That moment was captured by sculptor Jack Harman in a bronze statue in Vancouver.

Disappointments can easily control us in such a way that we constantly look over our shoulders. Regret or remorse or lost opportunities become a dead weight that paralyses us.

That is no way to win the race. We must forget what is behind and strain forward to what is ahead (Philippians 3:12–14). Look to Jesus. He has run the race before you and he will bring you safely home. Keep your eyes on the prize – look beyond the disappointments to all that Jesus is preparing for you:

> Therefore, strengthen your feeble arms and weak knees. 'Make level paths for your feet,' so that the lame may not be disabled, but rather healed.
> (Hebrews 12:12–13)

Trust Father; he doesn't make mistakes.

Questions

1. What does it mean to keep our eyes on Jesus? How does he inspire us to keep going?
2. Read Paul's testimony in Philippians 3:12–14 and his description of his hope in Philippians 3:20–21. How should being a citizen of heaven affect the way we behave today? How does it help us with everyday disappointments?

3. Think about the 'regret or remorse or lost opportunities' that may be holding you back. What do you need to do to put them behind you?

4. Read Revelation 7:9–17 and 22:1–5. How does John describe the 'infinite joy' that is offered to us?

Epilogue

Believe it or not, there are several islands that vie for the title 'Disappointment Island'.

However, the most popular candidate is an uninhabited one on the Auckland Island archipelago, about 180 miles (290 km) south of New Zealand. On 14 May 1866 the *General Grant* foundered a few miles off it. Sixty-eight passengers died. Fifteen survivors swam to the island where they waited for eighteen months before they were rescued. Their time there was so difficult that they christened it 'Disappointment Island'.

Of course, it's better than drowning, but would you really want to be stranded for any period in a place with such a name?

And yet there are many people who are long-term prisoners on their own Disappointment Island. They have got used to it and settled there. It's the new normal. But is that where God wants to leave us? The message of this book is that we all visit Disappointment Island from time to time, but we don't have to settle there!

Like every unpleasant thing in a broken world, the way we respond will determine the outcome. Disappointment can shatter our faith and wreck our Christian testimony. Or we can invest our experiences wisely. We can allow our disappointment to shape us and help us to value God's gifts without forgetting the Giver. It can drive us into the arms of God, as it finally dawns on us that he is the ultimate source of satisfaction and joy. It can make us homesick for heaven, where for ever there will be no disappointments. So loss becomes gain and growth as we see it in proper perspective, where it belongs.

One day Disappointment Island will disappear like Atlantis, and we will enjoy the glories of the new heaven and earth for ever. Edrie and I are looking forward to meeting Nathan when we get there. But more than that, we will gaze on the face of our Redeemer.

The apostle John paints an exquisite picture of this place of supreme delight:

I answered, 'Sir, you know.'

And he said, 'These are they who have come out of the great tribulation; they have washed their robes and made them white in the blood of the Lamb. Therefore,

'they are before the throne of God
    and serve him day and night in his temple;
and he who sits on the throne
    will shelter them with his presence.
"Never again will they hunger;
    never again will they thirst.
The sun will not beat down on them,"
    nor any scorching heat.
For the Lamb at the centre of the throne
    will be their shepherd;
"he will lead them to springs of living water."
    "And God will wipe away every tear from their eyes."'
(Revelation 7:14–17)

Notes

Foreword
1. C. S. Lewis, *The Last Battle* (Lion, 1980), p. 172.

Introduction
1. Isaac Watts (1674–1748), 'There Is a Land of Pure Delight' (1709).

1. Living outside the Garden
1. Often attributed to James M. Barrie (1869–1937).
2. C. S. Lewis, *The Lion, the Witch and the Wardrobe* (HarperCollins, 2014), p. 116.

2. The thorns remain
1. Adelaide A. Procter (1825–1864), 'My God, I Thank Thee, Who Hast Made' (1858).
2. John Calvin, *Institutes of the Christian Religion*, 1.11.8, trans. F. L. Battles (Westminster John Knox, 1960).
3. Martin Luther, 'The Large Catechism', *The Book of Concord*, trans. and ed. Theodore G. Tappert (Fortress Press, 1959), p. 365.
4. Tim Keller, 'How to Talk about Sin in a Postmodern Age' (The Gospel Coalition, 2017), https://www.thegospelcoalition.org/article/how-to-talk-sin-in- postmodern-age (accessed 17 August 2017).
5. Ambrose Bierce, *The Devil's Dictionary* (CreateSpace Independent Publishing Platform, 2015), p. 165.

6. L. M. Montgomery, *Anne of Green Gables* (Arcturus Publishing, 2017), p. 36.

3. Am I allowed to feel like this?

1. T. S. Eliot, *The Waste Land*, Part 1, lines 60–63, *The Waste Land and Other Poems* (Faber & Faber, 2002).
2. Paul Mallard, *Invest Your Suffering: Unexpected Intimacy with a Loving God* (Inter-Varsity Press, 2013), pp. 23–38.
3. William Shakespeare, *As You Like It*, 2. 7. 169.

4. 'Only seventeen years to go': when work frustrates us

1. Quoted in John Stott, *Issues Facing Christians Today* (Marshall, Morgan & Scott, 1984), p. 161.
2. Ibid., p. 162.

5. Only people make you cry: when relationships fail

1. John Bunyan, *Grace Abounding to the Chief of Sinners* (Evangelical Press, 1978), p. 123.
2. Pablo Martinez and Ali Hull, *Tracing the Rainbow: Working through Loss and Bereavement* (Authentic, 2005), p. 3.
3. Quoted in The Briarfield Chronicles, http://thebriarfieldchronicles.blogspot.co.uk/2012/08/why-passion-is-pure-in-charlotte-bront.html (accessed 21 August 2017).
4. See Genevieve T. Jennings, 'Singleness', http://eden-cambridge.org/resources/documents/app/resource/899/title/singleness (accessed 28 May 2017).
5. Michelle Graham, *Wanting to Be Her: Body Image Secrets Victoria Won't Tell You* (InterVarsity Press, 2004), pp. 96–97.
6. Andrew Peterson, from the song 'Dancing in the Minefields', on his album *Counting Stars* (2010).

6. Parents in pain: when our children break our hearts

1. Paul Tripp, 'The Biggest Thing Christian Parents Forget', https://www.paultripp.com/wednesdays-word/posts/the-biggest-thing-christian-parents-forget (accessed 22 August 2017).

7. Loving what Jesus loves: when church distresses us and leaders shock us

1. Martin Luther, *Luther's Works*, vol. XXII (Concordia Publishing House, 2007), p. 55.
2. Paul Mallard, *Invest Your Suffering: Unexpected Intimacy with a Loving God* (Inter-Varsity Press, 2013), p. 131.

8. The enemy within: when we are disillusioned with ourselves

1. See e.g. Tim Chester, *Captured by a Better Vision: Living Porn-Free* (Inter-Varsity Press, 2010).
2. Dag Hammarskjöld, *Markings*, trans. Leif Sjoberg and W. H. Auden (Faber, 1964), pp. 128–129.
3. 'Mr. Bunyan's Dying Sayings', http://biblehub.com/library/bunyan/the_works_of_john_bunyan_volumes_1-3/mr_john_bunyans_dying_sayings.htm (accessed 31 August 2017).

9. 'I'm the only one left, and they are trying to kill me': when even God seems to let us down

1. Peter Taylor, *Brits: The War against the IRA* (Bloomsbury, 2001), p. 265.
2. J. C. Ryle, *Practical Religion* (CreateSpace Independent Publishing Platform, 2017), p. 130.

10. His name is Toby: God is good

1. Marshall Shelley, 'Two Minutes to Eternity', *Christianity Today* 38 (1994), pp. 25–27.
2. Ibid.
3. Ibid.
4. Taken from the hymn, 'How Firm a Foundation, Ye Saints of the Lord', by John Rippon (1787).
5. John Murray, *Commentary on Romans* (Eerdmans, 1997), p. 314.
6. Giorgio Vasari, *The Lives of the Artists* (Oxford University Press, 2008), p. 327.

7. John Stott, *The Message of Romans*, The Bible Speaks Today (Inter-Varsity Press, 1994), p. 259.

8. Elizabeth C. Clephane, 'The Ninety and Nine', *Sacred Songs and Solos* (1874).

9. *The Works of John Flavel*, vol. 4 (Banner of Truth, 1968), p. 397.

11. The darling of heaven: Jesus is sufficient

1. Peter Lewis, *The Glory of Christ*, 2nd edn (Send the Light, 1969), pp. 3–4.

2. See Daniel Clark, *Dead or Alive? The Truth and Relevance of Jesus' Resurrection* (Inter-Varsity Press, 2007); Lee Strobel, *The Case for Easter: A Journalist Investigates the Evidence for the Resurrection* (Zondervan, 2014).

3. From a sermon by John Stott that I heard many years ago. Unfortunately, I did not make a note of the place and the date.

12. Gratitude attitudes: guard your heart

1. Martin Rinkart, 'Now Thank We All Our God' (1636).

2. Charles Wesley, 'And Can It Be that I Should Gain?' (1738).

3. Henri J. M. Nouwen, *The Return of the Prodigal Son: A Story of Homecoming* (Darton, Longman & Todd, 1994), p. 85.

4. Andrew Murray, *The Prayer Life* (Rough Draft Publishing, 2014), p. 41.

5. John Piper, 'How Do You Define Joy?', 25 July 2015, http:// www.desiringgod.org/articles/how-do-you-define-joy (accessed 25 August 2017).

13. Giving what we love most

1. William Rees, 'Here Is Love, Vast as the Ocean', trans. from Welsh by William Williams (1900).

2. Philip Yancey, *What's So Amazing about Grace?* (Zondervan, 2002), p. 232.

14. The power of hope

1. See Thomas Hardy, 'The Darkling Thrush', verse 1, line 5.
2. Charles H. Spurgeon, *Christian History* 29 (1991), p. 37.
3. C. S. Lewis, *Miracles* (HarperCollins, 1947), pp. 236–237.
4. J. R. R. Tolkien, *The Return of the King* (George Allen and Unwin, 1955), pp. 229–230.
5. C. S. Lewis, *The Weight of Glory* (William Collins, 2013), pp. 25–26.
6. Roger Bannister, *The First Four Minutes* (Sutton, 2004), pp. 215–216.